He Threw the Elephant
in the Bayou

HE THREW THE ELEPHANT IN THE BAYOU
Covenants Made and Covenants Broken: Stories and Poems about the Journey of Faith

Resource Publications
An Imprint of Wipf and Stock Publishers
199 W. 8th Ave., Suite 3
Eugene, OR 97401

www.wipfandstock.com

PAPERBACK ISBN: 978-1-6667-1318-3
HARDCOVER ISBN: 978-1-6667-1319-0
EBOOK ISBN: 978-1-6667-1320-6

07/19/21

He Threw the Elephant in the Bayou

Covenants Made and Covenants Broken: Stories and Poems about the Journey of Faith

Jody Seymour

To Clyde and Wanda many blessings Jody Seymour 8/16

RESOURCE *Publications* · Eugene, Oregon

All rivers have their source.
This book is dedicated to two of my sources:
my maternal grandmother, Hattie Smith,
and my mother, Esther Seymour.

Left: The author, Jody Seymour, with his great-great-aunt Hattie

Top right: Jody's maternal grandmother, Hattie Smith

Bottom right: Jody's mother, Esther Seymour

Contents

Acknowledgement

With gratitude to Gail Spach
for editing this book

Introduction

MOST OF THIS BOOK is about people you do not know by name, but as you read about them, you will discover some of your own past. The recollections come from my own memory bank of childhood days growing up in the country, between Biloxi and Ocean Springs, Mississippi. After recounting these stories from the past, I offer a few more about beginnings and covenants, and I close with some poems about the faith journey.

Some of the events depicted in this book I do not even remember. Some of the images were painted for me by my grandmother as I sat at her feet and baited her for more stories. The fishing hole of the past was full and I was eager to reel in as many of her memories as I could.

This book is about covenants made and broken. All of us make covenants, whether we talk in religious terms or not. If you buy a car, unless you are fortunate enough to lay down the cash up front, you enter into a covenant. Promises are made, papers are signed, and rituals are enacted.

It could be argued that covenants go beyond mere contracts. Covenants have a more personal quality laced into the agreement. Then again, personal is a relative term; some people truly love their car for instance. It is like a part of the family. Their payment book is a constant reminder of the covenant. Some people go as far as to worship the object of their covenant. Sacrifices are made to assure the constancy of the object desired. Most people think of covenants as personal bindings. Marriage is a covenant. Circumcision is a sign of an old covenant. Baptism is a sign of a new covenant

The last three stories do not come from my childhood. "If Ignorance Is Bliss, I Had a Blissful Beginning" is set just before I began seminary. It is about a broken covenant that made for a rather frightening start to what would become more than forty-eight years of ministry. "God's Yes!" has to do with covenant and childhood but this time, another child helps tell the story. "The Biggest Promise of All" simply recounts from a different perspective an understanding of covenant in the Bible. It is offered as a sort of overview of what it has meant for God to establish covenant with people.

The stories in this book mostly reflect grace and acceptance, sometimes gained through learning the hard way. In that sense, these stories may help you understand God's covenant with God's family. Oftentimes we are not aware of that covenant. It takes moments when life is thrown open in joy or ripped open in pain to remind us of how God is bound to the human family.

I hope you are reminded of your own childhood as you read these stories. We need to remember the joy and love of those days. We even need to take a look at some of the pain in order to learn something about who we are now.

I hope you enjoy the stories as much as I enjoyed telling them.

Jody Seymour

Part One

Recollections and Reflections

Home

WE HAVE ALL HEARD stories from our childhood and wondered in later life, do I really remember the event or have I heard the story told so much that I think I remember it? This is one of those stories. The memory is so much part of my soul that it does not really matter whether or not my mind is able to project the slide on the wall. I remember.

My mom and dad, Esther and Joe Seymour, were one of those typical post-World War II couples who had gotten married with no idea of what they were going to do next. Dad's family knew only about shrimping and surviving as best they could. Dad was to mom's family the guy from the other side of the bridge. Ocean Springs was only a few miles away from Handsboro, but the distance was great.

When his new wife suggested that he pull himself away from what she considered a restrictive lifestyle and go to college, it did not go over well with the Seymour clan. Mom and dad had gotten married without telling anyone from either family. That kept it simple for a while. When Hattie and Leon, mom's mother and my step-granddad, heard the news, they were not exactly happy either, but then, what was done was done. Families either take the new one in or they cease to be family. This family had been through enough not to entertain the idea of ceasing.

Ten months after the secret wedding, I came along. The doctor had told mom not to worry about birth control because as messed up as she was in the internal female department, there would be no children in the future. Doctors know only so much. I was evidently meant to be. When mom told me about my unexpected arrival, I put such vital information away to be used later at an opportune time.

The opportune time came the next day when mom became very angry with me for something I had done. I smiled and reminded her that I was, after all, "her little miracle." Surprisingly, the reminder seemed to work.

Unfortunately, young children do not know when enough is enough, so I tried the same tactic a couple of days later. I ended up in my room crying. The spanking I received was a bit more forceful than usual, probably because mom remembered how she had been taken in a few days before by information shared earlier.

Dad did go to college in spite of my unexpected arrival. Things were tough. Mom worked at a local store near the campus and came home in time for dad to go to class. Rumor has it that she wrote most of dad's term papers for him while he and many of the other GIs were out playing ball.

Dad got the degree. Mom probably learned more, however. They were both young and foolish like you are supposed to be when you are young and foolish. Like the drunk who somehow survives the unbelievable automobile accident because they were drunk and so "relaxed," young and foolish newlyweds need to be young and foolish in order to survive the sharp curves and wrecks that always come.

My memory, one of them, recalls that we had a car with no brakes. Dad would stop it by gearing it down. This meant that you pretty much had to know exactly what was coming your way so that there would be enough time to gear it down. Having heard my relatives recount the early days of my father's fathering, it was not only the car that had no brakes. Dad did not always know exactly what was ahead in a lot of things. Because of the way life was for many folks in the early 50s and because of dad's no-brakes attitude, our family ended up moving around a lot when I was a small child.

Here comes the kind of story that I "remember." We were at my grandmother's house and we were late to be off home. Families with no brakes usually are not on a schedule. Dad was trying to get me to get myself together so that we could take off. He must have been frustrated when he had to come find me for the third or fourth time from my hiding place.

The last time he found me, he screamed, "Jody, come on, we've got to get home!" There followed a pensive pause as I looked down at the floor and then looked back into my father's eyes. I uttered the now (to my family) famous words, "Daddy, where's home?"

Besides this story being on the menu of humorous stories that my family tells when they gather, I often think of these lines when I move. Being a Methodist Minister, moving is in my blood. Methodist Ministers, alongside circus people and military families, are a moving bunch. I have often wondered, where's home? Ask a Methodist preacher where they are from and they have to think a moment. Where is home? We have all heard the one-liners:

"Home is where the heart is."

"Home is where they always have to take you in."

"I'll be home for Christmas, if only in my dreams."

If home is where the heart is, then old St. Augustine would say that our home has something to do with God. Augustine once said, in a moment when maybe his daddy was looking for him, "Our hearts are restless until they find their rest in Thee." I have pretty much always possessed a restless heart ever since those no-brake days.

Travelers through life do have to find someplace though. So, where is home? Home has something to do with acceptance. It is the place where you gear down. It is the place where they take you in when your brakes fail.

If God is love, then home does have something to do with God. Home is where we learn about loving or where we do not learn and therefore remain restless until we find a place of acceptance and love. Home is about lost children being found. Home is where questions can be heard if not answered. Home is the place where memories are created and retold. Home is where the mind and the soul meet and remember together.

So even if you do not quite know the answer to "Where's home?" it is important that you ask the question.

The Wild Indian

NATIVE AMERICANS ARE A part of my heritage. I was told that my great-great-grandmother on my father's side was a Choctaw. But this story is not about my great-great-grandmother. It is about my grandmother on my mother's side of the family, Hattie, who became an Indian only because I named her so.

One morning, when grandma looked like any grandma would who had just awakened after a night's sleep, I managed to catch her with her hair let down, her makeup off, and all the trappings that come with humanity in the morning.

I informed her as only a child can, "Grandma, when you go to work you look fine, but when you stay home you look like a wild Indian."

That statement in and of itself is not particularly catchy or humorous (and may today not be considered appropriate), but my grandmother found it to be both, so it became one of her favorite stories and my nickname for her. She became for all time "the Wild Indian."

I tried one time to keep up with her on one of her jobs. She was a proof runner for the Daily Herald, the local newspaper in Gulfport, Mississippi. A proof runner is itself an interesting term. Would you think this would be a person who tried to get to the bottom of things? What is the real truth of this story? Let's get to the bottom of this.

Actually, a proof runner is the person who would take the proof for ads that were to run in the paper to the business or person running the ad. That person would then proof the ad to see if everything was okay and make any changes in the ad before the final copy was run in the paper.

Because so many people advertised in the paper, Grandma was known by almost everyone in the city. She was simply known as Hattie. Until the last few years of the job, she walked everywhere she went. It was on one of those days that I decided that I would follow her around. I was sort of like the puppy who at first enthusiastically stays close to its master on a long walk but soon starts lagging behind with its tongue hanging out.

I was supposed to be the young one with all the energy, but the Wild Indian could walk me into the pavement. She wore those old-fashioned granny shoes with the thick heels. They were always black and they looked to me to be very uncomfortable, but it was my feet that were sore at the end of the day, not hers.

When the Wild Indian retired from this job, it took two cars and three people to replace her. They do not make them like they used to, cars or people.

Grandma was the one I would go to in order to get to the bottom of the story. She was a proof runner for me. I used to love to sit at her feet and listen to her recounting of the past. The last time I was with her, I literally sat at her feet as she rocked in her chair, and I pumped her every chance I got for another story. She always responded.

She told me of the time that she became angry with me for not listening to her about rolling up the throw rugs. "Jody, when you roll the rugs up like that it makes them bunch up and people can trip over them. Don't do that anymore!"

Of course, that was an open invitation to do it again. After I was caught doing it again, I received a rather severe reprimand, so severe that I decided to retreat to under one of the beds. The Wild Indian was not about to budge. I could stay there for as long as I wanted. I was stubborn and thought surely she would come to fetch me. She was equally determined that I could remain in my dusty, dark retreat for as long as I wanted. She did come in to the room one time and put a glass of water next to the bed.

When Leon, my step-granddad, returned home from work, he noticed the glass of water sitting beside the bed. I was really afraid then because he was a big guy and I knew he would take grandma's side. He always did. He was also the one who, on another occasion, had told me to go back out and "pick up my own pencils" when I came in screaming one afternoon after my first-grade class.

I had dropped my box of pencils and crayons in the middle of the road when I heard the two dogs next door coming after me. They were always locked in a pen but this day they had gotten out. I could hear their paws quickly sweeping away the magnolia leaves as they rushed my way. I dropped everything and ran. They literally almost got my heels. Leon had no sympathy for a crying boy who was afraid of some dogs.

From that day on I figured he must not care if little boys got eaten up by mean dogs. It was of no use to come out from under the bed. For all I knew, he would pick me up by the ears and cast me into the magnolia leaves next door while he whistled, "Here boys, come and finish him off."

I stayed under the bed until my mother came home, according to the Wild Indian. Pleading my case to my mother did not help much. She must have talked to Leon. She took the Wild Indian's side too!

Grandma Hattie was sixteen when she got married. Bob, her first husband, was older. Sixteen-year-old girls should not get married now, and from what grandma told me, they should have not gotten married back then either. Girls should be allowed to be girls for as long as possible. They have to become women too soon anyway.

One of the reasons that my grandmother lived as long as she did, I believe, is that even at an advanced age she insisted on cutting her own grass. Her lot was over an acre, and she still used a push mower. People would fuss at her about cutting her own grass especially on those hot Mississippi days, but she kept on doing it. She would say that if she died behind the lawn mower, she would die active and happy. I liked that. I had been in too many nursing homes to talk her out of cutting the grass.

The Wild Indian collected people. There is no telling who you might discover if you dropped by her house. People knew that her hoops were broad. She had a way of finding the best in the worst people.

She was walking talking love. She was history in action, but she was most of all "the Wild Indian."

There need to be places where we can hide under beds when things get too rough. Those places must be where someone is there who will allow us to stay under the bed or who will be there for us if we want to come out and talk about it. In between times, a glass of water helps.

We also need people who are proof runners, people who can give us the bottom line when it comes to love, even if the bottom line is confrontational truth. Along with beds to hide under, and hoops to hide in, we all need people who sit in rocking chairs to slow us down enough to listen to the past, a past that can teach us something.

So, I thank my Choctaw ancestor, who gave me something which is somehow part of me, but most of all, I thank my Wild Indian, who gave me my personal history in so many ways. You kept on mowing as long as you could, dear grandma. When I first started this book, which has its origin in some of your stories, you were still with us.

Since then, I have done your funeral. I hope you don't mind that I told the Wild Indian story and some stories of my days of running proofs with you. The truth is I have told many stories about you in the many sermons I have preached. You are part of me and you will always be my Wild Indian.

He Threw the Elephant in the Bayou

THIS STORY, WHICH TOOK place before I was born, was told to me by my Wild Indian, my maternal grandmother, Hattie. Aunt Verna Mae, who appears in this story, is the wife of Sugarboy, the older of my mother's two younger brothers.

Ralph Green was a lover, at least as much of a lover as one could be in the ninth grade during the mid 1930s. Ralph had an interesting way of showing his love to those young Mississippi girls who were fortunate enough to become the focus of his attentions.

Through the ages, young men have given various objects to young women as a sign of their affections and intentions. Countless assortments of bracelets, pins, and rings have been the usual "outward and visible signs of inward and spiritual graces." Ralph transcended these rather everyday objects, whether by circumstance or choice. There is no documentation as to why Ralph made his selection.

A small white, some say it was ivory, elephant was Ralph's sign of covenant. If you were tops on Ralph's list, you got the elephant. This small handheld symbol became rather famous. Possession of it became a source of pride.

Whispers could be heard outside of humid classrooms: "She's got the elephant!" Perhaps the holding of the elephant became more of a game than a symbol of true affection for Ralph. That is of no consequence now. The elephant had become a symbol. Around this symbol there had formed a mystique. The elephant had become much larger than its tiny size.

Somehow my Aunt Verna Mae ended up with Ralph's elephant. Of course, back then she was no one's aunt. She was an attractive young girl of fifteen who in Ralph's eyes was fair game to receive the ivory object of affection.

This all would have been fine and good except for the inserted reality that my Uncle Sugarboy, who was of course no one's uncle back then either, had already laid claim to Verna Mae. The trouble started with the truth that Sugarboy never was much of an object giver. One had to know Sugarboy to know what his intentions were. Ralph evidently did not know Sugarboy.

Later, Ralph took away the elephant from Verna Mae in order to give it to another candidate. Verna Mae, whose heart really belonged to Sugarboy, should have let it go at that but found that for some unknown reason she felt a sort of emptiness at not having the elephant anymore.

Putting out the kind of vibrations that only fifteen-year-old pubescent girls can, Verna Mae let it be known that she missed the elephant. Someone could have, and perhaps should have, mentioned to Ralph Green the idea of purchasing another elephant. Ralph, however, sensed a very real truth: there can be only one sign of any covenant for the promise to be binding.

Somehow Ralph convinced the other girl to give him back the elephant. She was, needless to say, somewhat confused until she heard that the elephant's destination was Verna Mae's empty hand.

Ralph had created his own version of Mississippi Mud and he was waist deep in it. The point of crisis came when all of the parties involved found themselves on a boat in the middle of one of those lazy bayous. It was some kind of field trip.

Sugarboy had heard of the impending return of the elephant and turned the corner to see Ralph standing beside Verna Mae. Verna Mae looked at Sugarboy, Sugarboy looked at Ralph, and Ralph looked toward an approaching Sugarboy and pondered what to do next.

In a moment of confrontation, Ralph pulled the sign of promise from his blue jean pocket. After uttering a few words that need not be repeated, he threw the elephant in the bayou. There in front of all the characters who had become involved in Ralph's covenant making and breaking, Ralph Green broke his version of the sacred tablets. He had come down from the mountain and, like Moses, he had found things not to his liking. From the mountain to the sea is never really as far as it seems.

Ralph cast the sign of the covenant into the deep. He had had enough of the weight of a tiny, ivory elephant.

Promises can get you into trouble, especially if the promises are made in all seriousness, or even if they are not. Ralph found out that the middle ground left him in the middle of a bayou with no place to stand. Most of us have stood where Ralph ended up.

The Dwelling Place

EVER NOTICE HOW HOUSES get smaller the bigger you get? When I was a child, the house of my maternal grandmother, Hattie, was huge. When I saw it as an adult, it seemed modest. I know "they" say (by the way, who is *they*?) that this is all a matter of perspective, but I really think that somehow things shrink. It is just that they shrink in proportion to the rate of growth of the individual who is observing. How is that for a new physics?

My grandmother's house was a huge white box with an enormous front screened-in porch. It sat up on various piles of bricks so there was a great mysterious play space under the house. In this space, forts could be made in the dark Mississippi sand.

No one had yet told me of the possibility of snakes and other crawling creatures also sharing this space with me. It's a good thing. My kinship with Adam comes out strong when someone mentions snakes. As an adult, I look under this same house and wonder how I mustered the courage to crawl under the place and like it. Adults learn to fear. Children do not know any better.

The house was not just a house. It was a dwelling place, a dwelling place for many kinds of people. A lot of folks dropped by, people who seemed to really enjoy just being there for a while. I only lived there for brief periods of my life but even when I did not live there it felt like a dwelling place, not just a house.

In my adult professional life, I stumbled over why the above is true. When I was preparing a sermon on that famous passage of Jesus in which he says "in my Father's house there are many rooms," I discovered that the literal translation for "rooms" is dwelling places. The term means that Jesus was not just referring to empty places but places where there is an abiding presence. That's grandma's house all right.

The yard was special too. First of all, it was huge. Any kind of game could be played within the fence that surrounded this generous green acreage. Two or three football games could commence at the same time. Family reunions could be held and everyone could scatter and still have their own space. There were acres of shade under the old pecan trees. Sunshine could be had in all sorts of places.

If the yard became over explored there was always the old shed out back. It was one of those sheds that contained all sorts of mysteries. I was not supposed to go into it alone because of some of those mysteries. Obviously, I went into it every chance I got. Once in a while I asked if I could go into the shed with Leon, my step-grandfather, so I could ask him what some of the things were that I got to see or even mess with while I was alone.

This shed also made a great "hide-behind" for official games and those times when you needed to do something for which hiding was called for. Some other stories in this book will tell you what I mean. Suffice it to say for right now that like most children I started my list early of things that I needed to hide.

The Spanish moss that hung from the pecan trees made a great building material for forts. Limbs could be collected and moss gently placed over the limbs to create a kind of Southern igloo. These childhood constructions were wonderful, but one could not remain in them for too long. Even the natural "air-conditioning" was not enough to keep them from reminding children that it was hot in southern Mississippi.

Grandma told me in my adult years that after World War II she kept sixteen boarders. Now I know I said that for a child this house seemed big, but believe me, it was not that big. Where in the world sixteen boarders slept is a mystery to me. I asked her and when she explained, it still did not make any sense. What made even less sense is how she fed them all, and she did, three meals a day.

After grandma battled with cancer, her only daughter, my mother, had to take over the running of the operation for a while. The men had been spoiled for my grandmother Hattie always fixed their lunches for them to take to work. Each lunch was fixed according to each man's pleasure. When mom took over, she announced, "I don't want to hear any complaining. You'll be lucky to get anything at all with me packing you lunch." Nobody said anything. My mom had a way of declaring something to be so and it was so. I know.

Part One: Recollections and Reflections

If it is true that a part of us remains wherever we have been, it is no wonder that this house is a dwelling place. I was told it was originally built by an old black man. That was some ninety years ago. He was good at what he did for it stood for many years. His spirit, along with those of at least sixteen boarders and countless sojourners, were invested into this dwelling.

The place hosted everything from hog killings to wedding parties. It was remodeled, repainted, re-roofed, re-insulated, and revisited. It had an abiding presence within its walls.

Alcoholics came there to sober up. Prayer meetings were held where the evils of alcohol were listed.

Proposals were offered on the front porch. Divorces were agreed to on the back porch.

Countless babies were rocked. I was one of them and it was the place where I rocked my first baby, my cousin. It felt strange but good, as if I had been rocked there before, because I had. And significant death vigils were kept within the walls of this house.

Overflowing tables were spread and times were had within those walls when there was not much to put on the table. It was a house of wondrous contrasts.

I can still remember the feeling as my family approached the front of the house when I was a child. Even then, the house appeared to be waiting for me to come. It seemed alive. The massive trees that formed a tunnel as we approached the front porch seemed to be welcoming arms that beckoned the traveler to come.

Where are your dwelling places? One of the problems with modern life is that we have plenty of houses around but not enough dwelling places. We need to abide some more and not just pass through so many rooms. To share life in all its extremities is a way of building a dwelling place to be.

No wonder when Jesus offered those brief glimpses of heaven, he spoke of dwelling places. What I need to be aware of as I travel is that anytime I make a place a dwelling place, I do something a bit divine.

The closing book of the Bible says, "And I saw a New Jerusalem coming down from Heaven . . . and the messenger spoke and said, 'Behold the dwelling of God is with people.'" Did you know that we could actually make this moss-covered existence of ours a bit more heavenly?

What Happens Behind the Shed
Stays Behind the Shed. Unless . . .

I CAN STILL REMEMBER how massive the magnolia tree was that stood on the edge of my grandmother Hattie's yard. Its branches created a massive canopy that invited all who would come to play beneath its canopy.

Under that magnolia tree I established a "relationship" with a friend, whom I shall call Brenda. We were both six years old. I will not reveal Brenda's real name for word has it that she is now married with children. This means she has a husband who might not appreciate my sharing of these days of innocence. There is a chance that Brenda might be upset if she reads these words, but somehow, I think she will understand.

Brenda was the only person around for miles with whom I could play when I spent those long summer days at grandma's house. I do not remember how Brenda looked except that she was blonde and she was a she. Whatever stage of development I was in, I was starting to notice that shes were shes.

Part of my exploration of the world of wanting to grow up too fast was due to Brenda. She did not realize what she was doing, but she helped pull me into the edge of the adult world.

It all began that day I sneaked some Pall Malls out of the house. This was before the days of filtered cigarettes. I met Brenda literally out behind the shed. (Be patient, we have not reached the magnolia tree stage yet.) I lit up one of the cigarettes. Brenda watched. I felt big.

She did not want a cigarette. Brenda, even back then, must have possessed an innate wisdom. What she did do though caused me to suddenly step over into the real world of adults. After I had blown out a few puffs of smoke, Brenda said, "Suck it in like they do in the movies."

At this point, I had to act like I knew what to do. After all, I was a he and she was a she and hes had to prove their he-hood to shes, especially if you are six. So, I responded to her request by not just sucking in a little but a lot. I breathed in that refuse of unfiltered Pall Mall like I was trying to inhale the whole atmosphere of that delta Mississippi afternoon.

What happened next is either humorous or scary, depending on how you feel about smoking. When that mysterious cloud of big people smoke got inside of me, I do not know where it went. All I know is that it would not come out. You see, I'd had a glimpse of how they did it in the movies in terms of intake, but my knowledge ended before I got to the output.

I tried to breathe but there was no breath to breathe. I tried to force the smoke out but a roadblock had been set up and nothing could pass.

Brenda laughed.

In my effort to be a he showing off to a she, this was not the response that I had anticipated. At this point, however, her laughter was lost amidst my panic.

When she asked me what was the matter, all that would come out was a strange sound that emanated somewhere below my ribs. It was the sound of life trying to live.

I left Brenda behind the shed and ran into grandma's house all the while making that same life-grasping sound. My memory is foggy at this point, probably due to some minor brain damage or to a subconscious need to repress such a fearful moment. I believe that some adult in the house hit me on the back.

Whatever happened, after some primordial grunts, I did cough and breathe. The smoke of that Mississippi episode is still somewhere in my body.

All of this is just a lead-in to that afternoon under the magnolia. After this step into the adult world of cigarette smoke, I was ready for further exploration. Brenda and I were just old enough to realize that we were different. This sometimes leads to what is called by some as "playing doctor."

I found out years later from my grandmother that while Brenda and I thought we were quite alone under the magnolia tree, the ever-watching eyes of my grandmother observed what might happen if a six-year-old boy and girl were left alone too much. Two and two were added, and with the cigarette incident still present in the air like leftover smoke, it must have been determined that Brenda and Jody needed to play only in the presence of some big people.

It seems that what I thought "happens behind the shed stays behind the shed" was not true. Innocence, real innocence, lasts only so long. Adam and Eve, whom I had never heard of at the age of six, discovered the death of innocence under the branches of their own tree. I suppose that my wise grandmother, who did know the story, figured that after the shed incident and my quest to try grown-up stuff, it was the end of the age of innocence.

In my now grown-up world, I remember when our two teenage daughters pushed all kinds of boundaries in an effort to try grown-up stuff. I would often catch them in their efforts. I now know from some humorous recounting by both of those now grown-up daughters that most of the time I did not catch them. Which, come to think of it, is fine . . . now.

But when I did catch them, my comment was something like, "You might want to slow down. The grown-up world is not all that it's cracked up to be." My words were like grass seed that gets scattered onto the sidewalk: fertile but useless.

Ah but the analogy is apt, for some of those seeds eventually get washed to someplace where soil waits, or perhaps they get picked up by a passing wind where they find a place of rest and growth. I write this because those same two children who did not slow down are now in their grown-up world about which I warned. They now know the old man was right. How many of us would like to go back to a time of innocence where there were not so many decisions to make?

What goes on behind the shed of innocence does not stay there. We grow up too quickly whether we like it or not. What I should have learned behind that shed and perhaps under that magnolia tree, I must have forgotten. As I college student, like so many of my peers, I took up the adult habit of smoking cigarettes. And yes, I learned to suck it in like they do in the movies.

It was hard to quit, but after realizing that the first thing that second child of mine smelled when I picked her up and held her soft infant body to my chest was cigarette smoke, I took up running so I could quit.

Grown-up life is not all that it's cracked up to be. What happens behind the shed never stays behind the shed. The seeds find their way to a place of growth in the waiting fields of adulthood.

East of Eden waits just outside the bounds of the garden of innocence. Fig leaves give way to grown-up clothes and the sheds of childhood are only present in distant memories. So, Brenda, wherever you are, I hope you too can smile at our days of childhood exploration. I hope that life has been good for you and to you.

Ducking Pecans

PECANS ARE NOT MEANT to be weapons. That is why children should not throw them when someone is in the same yard. But children are children and I was a "children." I picked up one of those brown two-inch missiles and I hurled it toward my great-great-aunt, who I called Aunt Hattie (She was the aunt of my grandma Hattie).

I did not do this because I was mad at her. Quite the contrary, she was one of my favorite people. I was just playing around. How much damage can a child of five do with a pecan from such a distance?

The Philistines must have thought the same thing that day when they cheered on their hero, Goliath: what can such a small boy do with such a small weapon? You know how that story turns out, which goes to prove not only that right can overcome wrong, but also that children are not such bad shots after all.

My thrown-in-fun pecan landed squarely on Aunt Hattie's forehead. Squarely is not really the right word for it; if you have ever examined a pecan closely you will see that on one end of some pecans there is a definite point. I made my point.

What are children supposed to do when such points are made? I laughed. How funny it was that from such a distance I had hit Aunt Hattie with a pecan!

Aunt Hattie had always laughed before when I had lovingly hit her. She would even wrestle with me with her hands. I knew, even at five years of age, not to ask her to really wrestle with me because she was old. She was the only really old person I knew. My grandmother was not yet old, but somehow, Aunt Hattie seemed very old.

After my pecan found its mark, however, there was no laughter. Aunt Hattie just stood there. I think she must have been more surprised than I was. She too had not expected me to be able to reach such a distance with my playfulness. Like the horse paying no attention to the horsefly, Aunt Hattie had been allowing me my pleasure.

It was when the trickle of blood started easing down her brow that I froze. There we were like two pillars of salt that had just looked back. I was the first one to break this posture of surprise. I ran screaming toward her. By this time, she had realized what had happened.

Because she loved me so and because she had loved and lived longer than I had, she also realized that even in her dilemma she had to begin consoling a terribly afraid child who had just inflicted a wound on his Aunt Hattie. She cupped her hand over the gash and reached the other hand down to me, "It's okay, you did not mean to. I will be okay."

But I knew better. I knew she was old. I knew that old people disappeared often. I knew that when they disappeared that they did not come back. The big people called it death. I had heard the expression "bled to death." I knew that I had killed Aunt Hattie.

I was already having visions of my parents and grandma coming home and finding a screaming five-year-old standing over the body of a limp old woman. I could already hear the words ringing in my ears, "How could you have done this to your Aunt Hattie?"

There would be no explaining. No one would believe my story. How could a child kill someone with a pecan? Would anyone have believed David if the armies had not seen it for themselves?

I was thinking all of this as I was screaming bloody murder (wow what a use of terms). Aunt Hattie made her way into the house and put a washcloth over her injury. I was begging for her forgiveness while at the same time pleading with her to call a doctor. She kept assuring me that she was fine, but I knew better. I was five and I knew that old people were not supposed to bleed.

Aunt Hattie did recover. She did call someone, more to comfort me than to help her. A neighbor came over and helped her apply a cold rag. A tight Band-Aid and my calming down helped matters considerably.

All of this is to say I loved my Aunt Hattie. She had never had any children of her own so she adopted various others in the family. Since my mother and grandmother worked, it fell to Aunt Hattie to watch after me in that year before I was to start school.

Aunt Hattie shaped me. Oh, I know that is an expression we use of people who have influenced us, but in this case it was literally true. My mother later told me that when I was born, I came with a distinct point on my head. (Much like the point that is at the end of some pecans.) This point was the result of an unusually tough labor, according to my mother. It resulted in such statements as, "What's the matter with his head?"

Since this is not exactly the kind of comment parents want to hear when they bring a new baby home from the hospital, my Aunt Hattie took it upon herself to reshape things. She took the matter into her own hands.

Each evening while the other adults talked of adult things, my Aunt Hattie cradled me in her lap with a towel tightly but lovingly pressing against the top of my head. My mother said she would sing songs while I was in this vice grip of affection. After many songs and evenings in the rocking chair, things shaped up.

So, when I say Aunt Hattie shaped me, I mean it. Like ole Jeremiah the prophet discovered that afternoon in the potter's shed, the clay, even though it looks spoiled, can still be reshaped by a skilled potter.

Aunt Hattie was very possessive. After all, she was willing to spend her time shaping me, tending me, disciplining me, and all the rest. Why should she not tell my parents how I should in fact be raised?

One of the rules of the Universe is that no one else can tell another person how to raise their kids. It did not work this time either. Even at five I could feel the tension growing in my grandmother's home.

I felt sorry for Aunt Hattie then. I did not understand why the adults did not listen to her. She was older than they were and she loved me. What was the problem?

Revisionist history helps me understand that Aunt Hattie was all that I have described but she was also stubborn and deceptive in her ways. There were conflicts going on that I had no knowledge of. The house was growing too small for too many big personalities. It is a strange blessing, however, that love is blind and that children cannot see everything.

I lost track of Aunt Hattie. After I moved away to North Carolina when I was seven, I wrote her a few letters to which she always responded, but then the process of being a kid took over and I quit writing. Perhaps she found another adoptee. After some more conflicts, she moved away from the house of my grandmother Hattie to a place called Wiggins. The aging process did its work and she became bedfast and more stubborn.

I only saw her one other time, when we visited her some years later. A stroke had taken away the glimmer in her eyes. I was ten or eleven and tried in my own awkward way to communicate with her. I felt guilty for not having spent more time with her. I did not understand at eleven what a stroke does to a person so I interpreted the vacancy in her eyes when she looked at me to be anger for not returning some of the love that she had invested in me. I wondered that day if maybe she did remember that afternoon in the side yard when I hit her with the pecan.

Was the hurt because of that old wound or was the wound more recent? Had I hurled at her the cruel missile of neglect? From a distance had I thought I could not hurt her?

I cried beside her bed, not the same kind of desperate tears I had shed that afternoon in my grandmother's kitchen when I saw my Aunt Hattie's blood on the floor. Rather, I cried the slow tears of a young person learning the lessons one learns when the movement from childhood to adult begins to happen. I cried because I was confused. I cried because I knew it was too late to play in the side yard and make up for everything. I cried because Aunt Hattie would no longer watch me make crude houses out of Spanish moss and tree limbs that she could inspect after I had completed my work. I cried because I sensed I was losing something to death and I wondered if I had, like that afternoon years before, thrown something her way that was killing her.

Aunt Hattie did not die until a few years later, after she had been moved to a nursing home. I did not go to the funeral. I was older and too involved in the things that teenagers get involved in. Love had become a warm feeling coming from something that had to do with girls. There was very little room in my mind for remembering the past. The future was happening at an alarming pace and I did not want to miss any of it.

I hope somewhere in Aunt Hattie's mind, even in its limited capacity after her stroke, that she remembered how much I loved her and how easily children and youth get lost in their own world and forget. I hope she had within her that same understanding that was present that day a little boy hit her with a pecan.

So many people shape us. Some of those hands we can still feel touching us if we will stop long enough to remember. It is also appropriate to recreate in certain moments those times we have wounded the people we love. We do not need to relive those pictures just to feel guilty or sorrowful but in order to learn for the future. We touch many more people than we are aware we touch. We think we are at such a distance that maybe we cannot reach them with our intentional or even whimsical tosses. We are not as far away as we think we are.

Oh, Aunt Hattie, I remember. You are still teaching me. Even as I write these words, you are still shaping me. Sorry about the pecan and the forgetting. Please know that, now more than ever, I feel your loving hands.

Fresh Eggs and Fresh Graves

MAYE AND EARL WERE quite a pair. Maye looked like a female version of the Pillsbury dough boy and Earl looked like a walking skeleton.

Before moving to the house beside my grandmother Hattie, Maye and Earl lived beside the bayou. As a child, I remember the short trips out to their house to get fresh eggs. I think the trip was for more than procuring eggs. Maye and Earl were friends with my grandma, and the trip provided an opportunity to keep the relationship fresh.

The house beside the bayou has a place in my memory alongside some scene from an old movie. Entrance to the house could only be gained by a long winding dirt road that was itself a mysterious journey for a child. At the end of the road there waited all sorts of things to explore.

It felt like the past lived at the end of that road. Somehow going to Maye and Earl's was like traveling down a time tunnel; it was like living in another world. I never saw any chickens so I wondered where the eggs came from. Did someone from the past drop them off? Sure, they were fresh but from what era? There was something wonderfully strange about that place beside the bayou.

So it was that I was greatly surprised when Maye and Earl decided to build a house beside my grandmother. Why give up such a place of excitement and mystery? I did not ask and no one bothered to offer the information.

Even more fascinating to me was that when Maye and Earl came from out of the woods, they also became real live people. I discovered for the first time what these two people did besides sell eggs.

Earl was a grave digger. I know a child of five is not supposed to have great deductive skills but for the life of me I could not figure how such a frail man could possibly shovel dirt. Earl rather looked like a definite candidate for a grave to be dug for him.

Within his wrinkled face, there was one of the strangest smiles I have ever seen. Perhaps it came from being around so many dead people. Maybe the dead share a secret that is humorous, and only Earl knew the key to unlocking the secret. His smile was one that made the viewer wonder what was behind those narrow eyes and small grin.

I have a fresh understanding of Earl now. My first paying job when I was in high school was during the summer with the department of Parks and Cemeteries in the city where I lived. I became part of that select group known as grave diggers. My wife still does not desire that I begin my resume with this revelation, but I rather take pride in my four years as a grave digger.

You meet some really interesting people digging graves. To say that the folks who dig graves full time are earthy is not to make some bad joke. As a young, naive, pubescent lad, I was astonished at the stories my fellow grave diggers told me. I received a good deal of education in this strange "summer school." I began to understand why Earl smiled so much. Since I am one of the few initiated into the "planters in the earth society," I cannot reveal the secrets. Let it simply be stated that digging and covering up graves gives one a different perspective on life.

While Earl had dirt under his fingernails, Maye had dough under hers. Maye baked cakes for a living. I have never witnessed anything like Maye baking cakes. The phone would ring and some voice from somewhere would tell her how many and what kind of cakes needed baking that day. Then, the process would begin. Mixers would run, bowls would be filled with all kinds of stuff, and the kitchen would heat up. When it was all done, the counters would be covered with every type of cake imaginable.

At that time, I felt sorry for poor ole Maye. I knew how hard she worked to make these gorgeous cakes, and I figured that she could not receive much money for her efforts. I had never paid money for a cake, especially a home-made cake. They could not be worth much. It was only years later that I discovered how much people will pay for a custom, homemade cake.

Maye would load the cakes carefully into her car and make the trip to town. I used to worry about her because I kept imagining her having to suddenly put on the brakes and all her work ending up all over the car. Every available space in her car was covered with cake.

I used to wonder what Maye and Earl talked about at night. "How many cakes did you bake, dear?" "How many graves did you dig, dear?" When I was around them, they did not talk much at all. Perhaps Maye was unwilling to share any of her special recipes and Earl was unwilling to share the secrets of the graveyard. They had an arrangement, I guess.

When Leon, my step-grandfather, died, Maye baked a cake and Earl asked to be able to dig his grave. My grandmother gladly accepted the cake but would have none of the idea of Earl digging Leon's grave. She was concerned that Earl was just not up to it. I had thought that all along, except I had a suspicion that Earl was not up to digging anyone's grave. Earl later admitted that he was glad that grandma insisted. I was glad too, for I figured that every grave Earl dug brought him closer to his own.

Maye and Earl were living proof that two people can be different and still be meant for each other. One covered the hatching and the other the dispatching. One covered fresh stuff with icing while the other covered dead stuff with dirt. One seemed like fresh-baked, roly-poly love while the other seemed to be the sly keeper of the secrets of death.

But something kept them together. It was not the cakes or the graves. It was the unspoken bond that had nothing to do with cakes in the oven or bodies in the ground. Maye and Earl produced some children whose grandchildren I used to play with under the pecan trees that bordered the lot. They also produced some marvelous memories and questions for a young child who they let hang around.

Maye is now baking pie in the sky, and some unknown person has dug Earl's grave, but they are not forgotten. Every time I hear someone talk about needing to get some really fresh eggs, I remember. Every time I see some sidewalk bake sale, I remember. And every time I remember that the first job I chose was digging graves, I smile.

Waiting Arms

THE DAYS SEEMED LONELY for some reason. I am not sure why. Perhaps it had something to do with being an only child. In my grown-up years, I have done some reading about only children, and have discovered that we tend to see life differently from "regular" folks. Only children are victimized by the constant awareness that all of life should have something to do with how they feel at the moment.

Maybe I was lonely because I was a strange kid. Who knows? My parents never told me I was strange but then they were part of the reason I was strange, if I was. Friends were not going to tell me if I was different or strange. After all, five-year-olds are not supposed to be that self-reflective, are they?

The truth is, I was probably an ordinary kid, as ordinary as any five-year-old only child who had moved around constantly. I guess I had developed my own space that I took with me wherever I moved. Since that space was individually crafted by me, perhaps others did not feel comfortable in that space. How is that for hindsight psychoanalysis!

Whatever the reason for my solitude, it was not alleviated by the announcement that we were going to move again. This time it was going to be a major move, not just another local relocation. This time, dad was going up to a place called North Carolina. All I knew was that it was a long way from Biloxi, Mississippi, and that I did not want to move again. But, no one asked me.

Before I knew it, dad had gone "to prepare a place for us . . . and where he was, he would take us." Mom and I had to set up temporary residence at my grandmother's house. This meant living full time with Leon, my step-grandfather. Leon was one of those people who I knew for sure was not able to understand or share my space. This would be a challenge, for Leon and for me. Again, no one asked me.

I was enrolled at Mississippi City School after I turned six. I took my space to this new part of my world. I remember not knowing anybody. When I was told that the move to grandma's house would mean moving schools, I probably should not have been upset, but you see I had already become comfortable with a particular set of people I did not know. Now, I would have to meet a different set of people I did not know.

All the grownups talked about how convenient it was that the school was just up the street from the house. I did not care. It might as well have been miles away, for that is where my mind was most of the time when I was there. I still have trouble with the ABCs because I went to three different first grades and must have missed starting on the ABCs at each place. Throw this fact in with the reality that my mind was often miles away and you have the resulting only, lonely, child who does not know his ABCs.

I remember mom trying to make all of this better by buying me a new pair of blue jeans. This was the first pair of new blue jeans I had ever owned. Now this is not some poor-mouthing I am doing. I simply do not remember ever having new blue jeans up to this point. I think our family did a lot of handing down things. Since I was the only child in my immediate family, I had a great selection of hand-me-downs.

Perhaps the new jeans were my mom's way of tranquilizing me. I took my medicine. The effect was devastating.

I discovered the hard way that I was evidently allergic to whatever it is that is in new blue jeans if you do not wash them before you wear them. My first day in my new classroom I knew would be uncomfortable, but my mind kept telling my body that it should not be as uncomfortable as it seemed to be getting as the southern Mississippi day heated up. My legs at first began to itch. The itch soon turned to a slow burn. The burn turned quickly to a forest fire.

I guess I could have turned to a friend and shared what was going on, but you guessed it, there was no such person who I had let into my space yet. So, I burned alone.

Somehow, I made it through the day. I was too embarrassed to try to convey my dilemma to anyone, especially a teacher. The walk home was hell. I was told to walk since it was so "convenient" but who was to know that my outer layer of skin was to become part of the new blue jeans? Every step felt as if I was depositing a little more skin into the new jeans.

When I did manage to get home and peel the jeans from my legs, the sight was not pretty. The jeans coming off might as well have been sand paper. I do not know if new jeans are supposed to be as stiff as those jeans were that day after I took them off or if it was the body fluids that had been sucked out of my legs that made the jeans so brittle after they had dried into the fabric.

Mom cried when she saw what she "had done to me." She took it personally and felt like she had abandoned her parental responsibility by not washing the jeans first. I really felt sorry for her in spite of my weakened state. The only good that came from this jeans incident was that I missed two days of school.

Dad would call from "up north" and give us progress reports as to how the preparation was going. After what happened with my jeans and a narrow escape from two barking dogs on my "convenient" walk home from school one day, I was about ready to move again. There seemed to be some promised sense of security waiting in the upper regions where dad had set up shop.

So it was that the message came that mom and I were to come up and join dad for good. What really made the news exciting was that we were going by train. And not just by train but by one of those cars where you had your own bunk beds and your own bathroom and your own private window to watch the world go by.

The trip up was exciting. We ate in the dining car with linen tablecloths and all. I still remember that a coke cost fifty cents. Typically, you could buy a whole carton of them for fifty cents! I knew that I must be in the big time.

The closer we got to the mystical land of the north, the more I realized that I would have to create another space in another place. My shoulders started feeling heavy.

It was appropriate that when we pulled into the station, a dense fog covered the area. All that could be seen as I leaned out the door of the train were a few dim lights. There were no people to be seen. It was two o'clock in the morning to begin with. I did not expect a brass band to greet me at two o'clock in the morning but a few people would have been nice. After all, I at least wanted to know if people in North Carolina looked like people in Mississippi. Dad had not mentioned anything about how the people looked.

I stepped off the train into the cold December night. Mom, attempting to hold on to a bag, let go of my hand. She said something about staying close to her but her words faded into the fog as I saw a figure in the distance.

It was a solitary figure. I understood solitude. It did not really scare me. I had become rather comfortable with it.

I started walking toward the figure. About this time, my mother panicked. Here we were in some strange, fog-covered train station at two o'clock in the morning, and her only child was wandering toward some stranger.

She screamed for me to come back. I stopped. Suddenly, I realized what I was doing. Who was this I was walking toward? Fear then settled in with the fog. I turned and looked over my shoulder where I could barely make out the image of my mother.

It was then that a moment happened which is one of the pictures I have hanging on the wall of my soul. The outline of the solitary figure changed. Two arms reached out. There were no words. They were not needed. I saw the arms and I ran toward the arms.

My mother screamed all the louder for me to come back. I did not know what I was doing. But I did. No stranger would stand in the fog and offer outstretched arms. In my space, there was a vacant place that needed filling. That place was just big enough for the outstretched arms of my father. I ran into the fog. Only one time in my dash did a touch of fear make its way in. I ran through the fear just as I ran through the fog.

I still could not see his face but I could see the arms, open and empty. I melted into the coat of the figure with the open arms and only then did I hear my name. I was home. Even in the uncertainty and the lack of clarity of image, I was home. There were open arms and the figure knew my name.

We are all only children, no matter how large the family of origin. We are "only" in the sense that we all have a waiting father who knows our name. It is hard to approach that which we are not sure of. It takes a leap of faith, sometimes even a run of faith. Fear always accompanies our journey for we cannot see very far ahead. But if you look with eyes of love and faith you will see outstretched arms. That is the kind of father we all have.

We all need to be held, for nothing seems to stay the same. Like old Abraham, we are often called to move out from the place where we are comfortable, move out into the unknown. It can be scary. We may be chased by the wild dogs of life. We may even lose some of our skin. What will really keep us going is the promise that in the fog that often comes there is someone out there waiting with empty arms who will not be satisfied until those arms are filled with an "only child."

Waiting

WAITING IS SUPPOSED TO be difficult, but it is the waiting that makes what is being waited for so good. One of the problems with contemporary life is that we have to wait for so little.

If Jesus were teaching today, he would probably tell the parable of the microwave rather than the seed growing in the field. We are not willing to wait. We speed up seeds with nutrients and various fertilizers. After we rush the growth process along as much as possible, we shove the resulting product into the microwave so that we will not have to wait too long to consume the hurried fruits of our labor.

No wonder food has become for many a maintenance function. It is not surprising that we have trouble feeling satisfied. Our fast-food psyches do not have to wait. Since the longing-for period is so short, so is the satisfaction.

My grandmother Hattie's front porch is for me the image of waiting. It was filled with rocking chairs. Those chairs are seldom used now; they simply collect dust. One of them is in my attic. Once in a while back then, someone would plop down for a little rocking, but then either the traffic became too noisy, or the heat got too oppressive, and the would-be rocker would need to move quickly from the screened-in front porch to the air-conditioned house.

In my childhood days, before the proliferation of air conditioning, the front porch was the gathering place. A row of five to six rockers faced another row of rockers. At the end of the porch was a Sears Roebuck oscillating fan that supplied the "air-conditioning."

I can remember learning the fine art of waiting in those days of childhood. I would actually watch with amazement the movement of that fan. It was a wonder to me how the little wheel and tiny black belt made the fan go from side to side. Leon, my step-grandfather, knew the magic which would make the fan go only so far and then return. He could make some mysterious adjustment and the fan would follow a new pattern.

Leon took on a god-like quality as I watched him make these adjustments. He was the one who spoke to the fan and said, "Only this far can you come and no more." Leon could control the fan. He was also the one who, in all his tallness, looked down at me. From his white-haired perch, he spoke to me words of admonition: "Son, do not stick your fingers in that fan."

Leon, in this regard, controlled my movements too. "You shall go only this far and no farther." All of this was part of my learning how to wait.

On the front porch I had to wait to be grown up. I waited alongside those who were already grown up. They allowed me to rock with them. I was granted entrance to overhear some, although not all, of the grown-up conversations as we all rocked together as family. The family that rocks together stays together, simply because it takes time to rock. Rocking is not a hurried activity. You "sit and rock awhile."

Those persons rocking on the front porch always drank coffee. This at first mystified me since coffee was consumed in the midst of the Mississippi heat. I once asked one of the grownups why they drank hot coffee on hot days. After receiving one of those looks that kids get when they intrude into grown-up assumptions, I was told that drinking something hot when you are hot actually cools you off.

I was a kid. They were big. I believed it. In the midst of my waiting to be grown up, I created my own version of coffee so that I could rock and drink with the grownups. This liquid mixture consisted of four parts milk, three parts sugar, and one part coffee. But it was in a coffee cup and I made sure that no one saw me fix it, so what did they know?

In my waiting I would rock and talk and sweat trying to believe in the assumptions of the adult world. Even at that young, tender age, I wondered what would be the harm of iced tea, but what did I know? I was just a kid waiting to be an adult.

I also remember those moments when I waited alone on the front porch. My only companion was the fan, whose movement seemed to keep me company.

I would wait for Richie and Susie, my cousins. Nothing is as lonely as a kid at grandma's house with no one to play with. I had left my playmates up in North Carolina, which was now home. The summer trips to grandma's house on the coast of Mississippi were tough for a kid who wanted to play and yet found himself having to wait to be grown up.

Richie and Susie were around my age. They lived down the road a few miles from grandma's house. They lived just far enough away to be away.

I would sit by myself in the evenings and look from my rocking chair off into the distance. A pair of car headlights would appear coming down the road that led to the front porch. I would hope that behind those lights would come the companionship of my two cousin playmates. Most of the time the headlights would stop for a brief moment at the stop sign and drive off.

My heart would beat a little faster the nearer the lights came. You can imagine the feeling when the lights would stop and then cross the road and pull into my grandma's front yard. The waiting was over. I would try to act a bit grown up when Richie and Susie appeared. After all, I was a "grown up in waiting" who had learned to drink coffee. But my waiting would soon give way to joy and play. The waiting made simple cousins into answered prayers.

We all need to wait some more. We have air conditioned too much and left the front porches of our lives. We do not take time to watch the oscillating movement of life. We may have forgotten how to wait. Could it be that is why life sometimes does not feel full? Could it be that we no longer think that life is worth waiting for? We need to take some time to sit and look down the road. We need to feel the waiting and anticipation that comes with the waiting. Padded recliners have become a symbol of a passive kind of waiting. Perhaps we need to find at least one old rocker and sit and rock a while and do some active waiting, the kind of waiting that anticipates something.

Jesus said that the Kingdom of God has something to do with being like a child. What I did not know as a child is that the longed-for adulthood that I so much wanted would hinder me from child-like waiting that leads to wonder and joy.

Find a chair. Rock awhile. Wait.

Paw Put

ALL THAT IS LEFT is a vacant lot framed by arching pecan trees. His house has been torn down to make room for the new highway.

The trees look lonely as if they are watching for Paw Put. Family tradition has it that I named my grandfather on my father's side, John Narcisse Seymour, this unsophisticated name of Paw Put. Somehow, in a language that only young children possess, I came out with something that sounded to listening adults like "Paw Put." Who knows what I was really saying?

Back to the lonely trees. I think they are lonely because Paw Put helped them grow. He used to spit tobacco juice on their exposed roots. He never said that he did so to help the trees grow but to a young child, what else could be the reason?

The house itself was stained a muted shade of red. There was a narrow front porch that was mostly unkempt, like the rest of the house. There was no woman's touch at Paw Put's, for my grandmother, Clara, had died years earlier, and along with her died the last reason to keep things ordered and clean. Paw Put would lean back in an old rusty metal chair with his feet on the porch rail. He could spit some of that special fertilizer toward one of the waiting trees from this position.

Paw Put was a full-time grandpa when I knew him. He did what grandpas were supposed to do. He hid candy in the linen closet. This candy, he said, was reserved for me only. The other grandchildren were around all the time. He could not keep enough candy to supply everyone so the candy in the closet was just for me on my infrequent stops at his house when my family made our summer journeys to Mississippi.

The idea that this candy was only for me made it taste especially good. I often wanted to tell my cousins about the special candy so as to assure them of my status, but I knew I would lose in order to gain. Besides, I did not want to get Paw Put in trouble. He had to live there.

Part One: Recollections and Reflections

There were a lot of grandchildren. These were Cajun Catholic folk who believed in big families. For an only child, I could not understand the reason for so many children, far too many to share candy with. The names of my uncles who were responsible for this proliferation of children sounded strange to me: Ulysees, Foster, Bernell, and one that sounded fairly common, Hubert.

Foster was the one who was the "individual" among the brothers. He knew how to drink and how to shrimp, in that order. He also knew how to cuss. I was a bit afraid of Foster, mainly because of his glassy eyes and his strange sort of smile that managed to show in the midst of his sandpaper beard.

Foster mumbled a lot. One particular mumble has become rather famous within our family traditions and has somewhat vindicated Foster in all his craziness. He mumbled this particular statement one afternoon on the front porch. It had been a long day on the shrimp boat and Foster, as usual, had stopped by the local watering hole that was conveniently located near the dock at the bayou where he parked his boat.

Refreshment had made Foster reflective, so he leaned over the porch rail and announced, "You see that swamp over there across the road? Somebody ought to buy the damn thing cause someday they're gonna build a fancy housing development right in the middle of it."

The vacant lot with the lonely trees is now bordered by Foster's prediction. Who knows what other prophecies Foster made that someone should have noticed?

Paw Put did not notice. He was busy being Paw Put. His pants hung down below his navel and he found no special reason to pull them up. He often had tobacco juice stains on his clothing. I did not care and it was obvious that he did not.

In his bedroom was a fireplace. The few times I made the trip down south around Christmas time, I got to sit in front of the fireplace. It was one of those fireplaces that was completely on the floor. Tobacco juice marked the trail toward the fire. The juice hitting the fire made a mystical hiss that I can still hear.

Paw Put yelled at the other grandchildren. He never yelled at me. Before I knew the phrase "familiarity breeds contempt," I figured it was because, like the hidden candy, I was special.

I do not remember much of what Paw Put said. He did not say much to begin with. It was the acceptance and the smile that I remember. Like Alice in Wonderland's Cheshire cat, a lot fades but the smile remains.

Paw Put let me play. What my mom and dad did not know was that he let me do most anything I wanted. He knew that I knew he was there so he let me go out and do most anything. Part of that anything included unlocking the shed, again only for me, and letting me drive the huge yellow Shriner's car that was stored there waiting for some parade that never seemed to happen. Gosh, did I feel big behind the wheel.

Before you think too harshly of my permissive grandpa for allowing a child to drive a car, you need to know one small item. There were no keys to this yellow chariot. My driving consisted of trips that I would take while the wheels never turned. I would adjust the knobs on the radio, and in my mind the music and the trip would commence. While at Paw Put's house, I traveled thousands of miles. My self-esteem was always greatly enhanced by my secret trips. The rest of the kids never knew what my smiles meant.

I heard Elvis Presley for the first time on Paw Put's front porch. Every time I hear "You ain't nothin' but a hound dog," I think of Paw Put. I am not sure he would be pleased by such an association but again, we were allowed to listen to such music on the porch of acceptance. Paw Put also introduced me to something besides driving, loud music, and special candy. He introduced me to death.

The long trip my family made to Ocean Springs when I was eight or nine was not to have me run across the porch into his waiting arms. It was rather to view for the first time someone lying in a metal box. Back in those days it was the tradition to allow children to kiss the deceased goodbye. I do not know about the therapeutic value of such a ritual of parting, but I know it scared me.

Paw Put had always smiled back when I kissed him. He usually seemed a little bit uncomfortable with me kissing him, but you guessed it, he allowed it. This time however, hovering over his coffin held up by the arms of my father, the grace seemed all gone. Paw Put was as cold as the swamp was black. The smell of tobacco juice was replaced by a strange smell, which I assumed was the smell of death.

This was also the days when all of the Catholic liturgy was in Latin. Beside my first graveside, I witnessed the surreal scene of a man in a white and black robe uttering strange and morbid sounding words while he scattered water from one container and swung smoke from another.

Even if this had not been my Paw Put, I would have wanted to protest. What a way to end the life of a man who hid candy, fertilized trees with love juice, and put me in the position to take my own road trips. It just was not fitting.

I would rather have seen Foster spit some of his own juice into the waiting soil to affirm life. I wanted everybody to quickly leave that strange place of death and hurry back to see the quite alive pecan trees. I wanted all of us to pile in that wonderful yellow car and start it up, really start it up, and ride down the road telling the beautiful stories of Paw Put and the grace he bestowed.

As we left that strange smelling place with the touch of incense hanging heavy over our souls, I thought even then, "Something's not right." I have learned in my grown-up years that one is supposed to feel not right at the edge of death, but this was too much not rightness. We went back to Paw Put's house after the funeral. While all the people ate some food, I quietly went into Paw Put's bedroom and found the place where the candy was hidden.

We all need acceptance. We all need permission to take our own road trips. We all need to take time to touch the trees, one way or another. And we all need to be able to find a little candy left behind by those who love us when we have to say goodbye.

Slap 'Em Upside the Head

I WAS THE COURT jester. Behind every clown there is a melancholy character trying to survive. I evolved into the class clown in my elementary school days. So much so that when our sixth-grade class was stuck with the duty of performing *Ivanhoe* it was natural that I was chosen to play the part of the court jester.

Mrs. Meiseimer, my sixth-grade teacher, did not like me being the court jester. Mrs. Meiseimer did not like me. I got all the laughs. I think she was jealous. I talked too much and when I did, people laughed. She did not like the idea that such a dramatic part might affirm my place as the class clown. She ended up writing in the comment section on my final report card, "Jody will never amount to anything unless he quits showing off."

What this frowning lady did not understand was that behind the court jester was a chunky kid who was trying to cover up some childhood pain and insecurity. I acted like I was pleased to be picked as the court jester in the play, but on the inside, I was sad, the same kind of sad I felt when all the girls sent me the Valentine cards that had elephants on them.

My nickname was "Rollaway," because I had caught the game-winning pass in an intramural football game. I had tripped, taken a forward roll on the ground, and then the ball landed squarely in my gut. The quarterback came running down the field after the pass completion screaming, "That-a-way Rollaway!" It stuck.

I laughed as all my companions patted me on the back and chanted "Rollaway, Rollaway," but it was not really funny. I wanted regular Valentine cards. Why could I not be Ivanhoe instead of the court jester? Why could I not have been carried on the shoulders of my teammates and given the game ball instead of being shackled with another comedy title?

Ivanhoe was a blast. It was probably the funniest production that Frank B. John Elementary School had ever witnessed. The problem was that *Ivanhoe* was not a comedy. Mrs. Meiseimer did not laugh. She was terribly embarrassed at what happened. That pleased me because the play really was funny.

Every mess-up that could have happened did happen. I set the tone when I walked out on stage in my home-made court jester outfit. I was supposed to say a very serious line to open the play. The line was never heard because of the laughter. Again, I was the clown. A pudgy court jester with bloomers on and a pointed hat dangling from my head simply brought the house down. I did not have to "jest," all I had to do was stand there. My contemporaries were grabbing their midsections and laughing uncontrollably.

The play degenerated rapidly after this standup comic entrance. Between forgotten lines and props that fell off the stage, the laughter continued.

The climax came when Stanley Berkshire, who was supposed to shoot a rubber-tipped arrow off stage left, ended up shooting Ricky Smith in the stomach. Ricky, who had no lines and was supposed to just stand there acting like one of the king's guards, grabbed his stomach and acted like he was dying. God, was it funny! Stanley, who had a great laugh anyway, turned to the audience and beamed. It was great. Mrs. Meiseimer died along with Ricky.

After the play, Mrs. Meiseimer thoroughly chastised us for the most ridiculous performance that she had ever seen. This speech, however, was somewhat diminished by the parade of messengers who came from various classes telling Mrs. Meiseimer and our class what a great play it had been. The real clincher came when one of the teachers told us how original it was to do a comedy spoof on *Ivanhoe*. I loved it. At last, my friends were laughing with me and not just at me.

My evolution into court jester really began in the first grade. Having moved twice within Mississippi and the third time to China Grove, North Carolina, I was in my third first-grade class. That is enough to cause some insecurities. Matters became worse the afternoon that a teacher told me to get in line with her class after we had finished recess. Evidently, she had mixed me up with some other new kid. I told her that I was in another teacher's class. She screamed something at me and told me not to sass her and to get in line. I knew that if I stayed in her line, I would end up in the wrong class so when she was not looking, I got back into the right line.

As the lines were filing into the building, she noticed that I had switched lines. She came running over my way, grabbed me by the arm, and slapped me upside the head. I lost my balance and fell over one of those knee-high rails that was positioned at the intersection of two sidewalks to keep people from cutting corners. I picked myself up and tried not to cry. She pulled me over into her line and told me to shut up.

Sure enough, I ended up in the wrong class. A few minutes later, my real teacher came looking for me. I thought for a few moments the "Gestapo" lady was not going to release me, but she did. There was no mention of any mistake being made. She stuck by her guns that I had sassed her. My new teacher gave me a lecture on listening to what teachers said even if they were wrong.

Thus began my "show-off" career. I figured I better get some laughs out of all this pain. I became good at it. I liked the attention and besides, since I was chubby, laughter was a good cover up.

Ole Rollaway bounced along pretty good until the fifth grade. I had moved again, this time to Frank B. John School in Salisbury, North Carolina. I had established my reputation as clown and things were going pretty well until Mr. Amendable, the Physical Education teacher, did not show up one day for recess.

Another teacher, the greatly feared Mrs. Judd, ended up with a whistle in her mouth trying to conduct a soccer match. Mrs. Judd was not my teacher, but I had heard of her reputation. She was mean and she looked it. I was the goalie for our team. When she gave a penalty kick to the team that had committed the penalty, I just could not stand it. I ran up to her and shouted, "Mrs. Judd, Mrs. Judd! That's the wrong way to do it!" She had been told this a number of times and her face was already red from the heat and accusations. She pointed her finger at me and told me that if I said one more thing to her, I would be sorry. I limped back to my goal.

The score was tied. I knew it was about time for recess to be over. The ball and the action were on the opposite end of the field. There was no one around with a watch except for Mrs. Judd, who was standing on my end of the field looking tired and disgusted. I left my goal and ran up to her. I was going to ask her how much time we had left in recess. "Mrs. Judd, Mrs. Judd . . ." I never got out the request for the time. She turned and screamed into my face, "That does it, young man." She pushed me up against the fence that bordered the playground and slapped me upside the head four or five times.

It looked like something on TV. I was the criminal who had been caught, and Mrs. Judd was the cop beating me up. All the kids on the other end of the field froze as they watched Mrs. Judd lose her cool on me. Again, I did not cry. I was too scared to cry.

We marched back into the building. No one said anything to me. I think they were scared too. What had I done to Mrs. Judd to arouse such anger? I was afraid even to tell my parents. After all, I remembered my third first-grade teacher's strange counsel: "Teachers are right even if they are wrong." I had been zapped by this strange truth again.

My clowning around was greatly subdued for a while until a few days later when a knock came at the classroom door. My teacher pointed toward me and called me to the door. It was Mrs. Judd. O my God, she had come to finish me off. She was going to destroy the evidence.

She looked down at me as she said, "Come with me." We went down the narrow stairs that led to the empty cafeteria. It was a perfect place for her to finish me off. There would be no witnesses. She told me to sit down. I sat down waiting for the blows to begin.

She sat immediately across from me and started folding a plastic bag which she had evidently used for her lunch that day. As she folded the bag smaller and smaller, she talked. I was afraid to look her in the face. I stared at the bag and watched it get smaller. Her words caused me to look up. She was nervously apologizing for her actions. She told me she had no right to hit me in the face and that she was sorry.

What? A teacher was sorry? A teacher was wrong? The bag which had started as a good-sized bag was now about two inches square. Somebody had gotten to Mrs. Judd. Some parent had been told about how she had beat me up on the playground. I figured she had been told by some official to apologize to me or else.

It did not matter to me. A teacher was wrong. I had been vindicated. I was free to be a clown again and would not get beat up for it.

All of this was part of the reason that Mrs. Meiseimer and I did not get along. My identity had been formed out of necessity, but she did not know that. She thought I was simply showing off. I was showing off, but there was a reason for my clowning around. The jokes covered up the pokes, so to speak. We all wear masks, do we not? Perhaps we wear them because we have felt slapped around a bit. We are afraid to show our true colors for fear that they will not be appreciated.

The "arrows of outrageous fortune" do not always fall off stage. Sometimes, they accidentally hit us in the gut. Some of us have learned to laugh rather than to cry. That is not all bad. The jester costumes we wear serve a purpose. But many of us need to be able to walk on stage and say our lines and be heard.

Well, Mrs. Meiseimer, wherever you are, you were right, but you also were wrong. I was a show-off, but it was so that I could amount to something. We all need to show off who we really are so that we do not have to wear too many costumes to become something we are not. Life often slaps us upside the head while we are trying to find out who we are. And yes, we sometimes get out of line. What Mrs. Judd needed to know was that the process of self-discovery sometimes takes longer than you think. You can't slap things into shape. It takes time.

I still like to show off. I think growing up means simply learning appropriate times to show off who you are. The reason God put us here together and not alone was so that we could help each other discover who we really are apart from the nicknames and the costumes.

Whom Shall I Fear? I Have a List!

MY FATHER WAS A man often filled with anxiety. The apple does not fall far from the tree; I possess the ability to become anxious, and quickly so. Dad once confided in me in his later years, after the death of my mother, that he suspected that the source of his anxiety and fears was the deep-felt remembrance that his mother seemed not to really care for him. In my years of study, I have discovered that this phenomenon can be called emotional abandonment.

Whatever the source of dad's battle with anxiety, his faith was not much help to him early on. He was raised Catholic, and the version of Catholicism he experienced came through the veil of incense, Latin chants, and a good measure of guilt.

Implanted in my memory is when all this changed. I was eight years old. Mom and dad had had some kind of verbal altercation, and in an effort to appease my mother, dad reluctantly agreed to attend a Billy Graham crusade.

We sat on the back row of the old Charlotte Coliseum. Then it happened. Billy gave his customary invitation. I was not paying much attention, but suddenly my father got up and started toward the steps. I assumed he was going to the bathroom so I followed since it felt like a good idea for me too.

We passed the turn for the bathroom and it was then that I realized that my father was headed toward the crowd that was standing in front of Billy. With "Just as I am" being sung in the background, I looked up toward my father's face. He was crying.

Later we were escorted back to an area where counselors were waiting to listen, offer next steps, and give us some initial written materials. The counselor had some for me too, geared for children.

That was the beginning of the journey. Dad switched from being a Catholic to become a Methodist so he could "be with his family." I remember he got a letter from the local priest cautioning him that "his soul might be in danger of Hellfire." (By the way they do not do such things now, but that priest long ago did.)

Our very mild-mannered Methodist minister assured my dad that he was going to be fine. All this is to set you up for what I am about to share with you in light of where we often find ourselves during difficult times. My over-anxious father morphed into a man who wanted to start faith-sharing groups. In some of the materials that Billy sent us, my dad must have encountered Psalm 27.

He wrote his own version of the Psalm because somehow it transformed his life. He had his version printed on rose-colored cards. I can still see those cards in my mind's eye. He handed them out at church and in the different groups he attended. Psalm 27 begins: "The Lord is my light and my salvation; whom shall I fear? the Lord is the stronghold of my life; of whom shall I be afraid?"

Whom shall I fear? In my opinion there is plenty of fear and anxiety to go around, but the same message of hope and comfort that my dad received comes through to me as I contemplate this Psalm. It could be that I'm being channeled by my deceased father or maybe it is the Spirit we call Holy. I am reassured by the words that appear later in the Psalm (verse 5): "For He will hide me in his shelter in the day of trouble; he will conceal me under the cover of his tent, he will set me high upon a rock."

Dad, I am glad you got up out of your seat that night. I am glad you found that Psalm, or perhaps that Psalm found you. In the tradition of my dear father, I now offer my version of this Psalm:

O Lord, you are our light, and I'm sure glad because it's dark out there.
It's sometimes hard to trust when it's dark, but the darkness is as light to you.
But, and you already know this, the dark is still dark to us.
So I am going to have to do what I sometimes do not do well:
I am going to have to lean into you and believe you will catch me when I fall.
It seems you are really good at catching, since your children seem to fall a lot.
But your arms are steady and strong when ours become weak.
I ask boldly for you to give us the strength we do not have.
You know our limits and we've reached them.
You are so much bigger than our fears.
One of your children wrote long ago,
"Wait for the Lord; be strong, and let your heart take courage;

wait for the Lord."
So Lord, we are waiting.
Thanks for always waiting on us.

If Ignorance Is Bliss, I Had
a Blissful Beginning

THE BRIEF VERSION OF my personal history has one of my "beginnings" occurring one evening when I was seventeen. I wanted to date this girl, but it was a school night and the only way I was allowed out was to go to church. Conveniently there was this youth rally being held at the large Methodist Church downtown.

The place was packed. My date sat beside me, and beside her was one of my best buddies. To make this very long story short, I had a vision. That is the only way I know to put it. The preacher got to me, somehow. He had us close our eyes and hold out our hands palms up. He then said something like, "I know this may seem and look foolish but remember, everybody has their eyes closed so it does not matter. Now I want you to ask Jesus to take your hands and lead you through life."

Well, okay, I did it. I had this funny feeling and then suddenly I felt someone's hands touch mine. I thought it was my date fooling around, so I cheated and opened my eyes as I looked in her direction. There she was, eyes closed, and hands extended. Beside her was my buddy in the same posture. It was then that, well, I guess you could say "the fear of the Lord" came over me.

I looked in front of me and there were two hands holding mine. I saw them and I felt them. I closed my eyes and began to tear up. What in the world? It was then that the preacher said, "Some of you may want to come to the altar." I needed to get away anyhow so that my date would not see the jock who asked her out all weepy eyed.

I went to the altar still crying and said something like, "Okay, you got my attention. I've had many people say I ought to be a minister but that's not what I have in mind, but if you want me that bad, I'll do it." Such episodes like I had are called mountain-top experiences. They are powerful, usually very individual, and fade with time.

So, I went to college all psyched up to be a minister, still living off the leftovers from the mountain. Then came a kind of famine that occurred not because I was too empty but because I was too full. I became fascinated with the study of religion, which may sound good if you plan on becoming a minister, but what happened was that it did not take long for all that knowledge to zap what I discovered was a very simplistic Sunday School kind of faith.

Before I knew it, between all kinds of philosophy courses and in-depth study of the Bible and religion, I could neither prove that God existed nor that I even existed. To say I was a confused young man would be an understatement. I did not yet know that what I was experiencing was pretty normal for a naive pre-ministerial student who had never really studied the finer points of religion and philosophy.

Here I was preparing to go to seminary and did not have anything in my saddlebags for the trip. My "God" had been too small and my faith too anemic. I had not yet found a replacement for my now-deceased childhood deity and was in between dried-up faith and the need to find a well.

I had to make a decision, and even though my mind was in a whirlwind, something would not let go of my heart, wherever it was. I guess it was those hands.

Now comes the "beginning in ignorance" that is alluded to in the title of this chapter. I was for sure full of new knowledge, but I would quickly discover that when it came to being a minister, I was going to discover a whole new level of what ignorance meant.

It all started when I agreed to do a Duke Endowment Summer Internship the summer before I went to seminary. The money was good and I was assured that the expectations for a new seminary student who had not even been to class yet would be minimal.

I was newly married and overly confused, but I went. When I got a short letter from the minister to whom I had been assigned, it seemed that he might expect more than I had bargained for. After contacting the Endowment Office about my concerns, I was assured that they had the contract in front of them that stated that I was to "work with the youth, help with Vacation Bible School, read the Scripture for Sunday morning worship, and help out around the church."

So, my new bride and I pulled up in the driveway of the parsonage and discovered a man packing a car. The trunk was open and full. As I got out of the car, the man said, "You will be staying in the parsonage so let me show you where the fuse boxes are because we have a lot of lightning storms around here."

As I followed him, I said, "Who are you and where are you going?" He turned ever so slightly my way and said words I will never forget: "I am the preacher but I am about to have a nervous breakdown. My wife has been going to the Baptist church because she can't stand the people in my church. We have sublet a motel at the beach and will run that for the summer. The Lay Leader will come by tonight and take you and your wife out to eat. Oh, and by the way, I know you were told that there are two churches on this charge, but at Conference they added another church so now you have three."

I have three? What did it mean I have three? Who has three? Surely not me? I am here only to "help out." Well, he did show me where the fuse boxes were, and then I followed him back to the car. He gave me the keys to the parsonage and said, "I hope you have better luck than I have. I'll be back after your ten weeks are up."

He got in the car and drove off. I cannot express the feeling I had. So, who is it that I am supposed to "help out"? I wondered.

Later that evening, after my also-in-shock wife helped me unpack, a short round man and his wife showed up to take us to Parker's Barbeque. After some food and small talk, we found ourselves back at the parsonage. As he started to leave, I asked him, "Mr. Applewhite . . ." He stopped me and said, "Call me Jim Bill." "Okay, Jim Bill, well, it is Saturday night and I was just wondering who will be preaching tomorrow?"

He smiled and slapped me on the shoulder and said, "Well, that would be you since you're the preacher. See you in the morning! You preach at our church downtown every Sunday, and in addition to that, you'll alternate between the other two churches each Sunday."

Then he was gone. I looked over at Betsy and did not even have to say, "What in the world is happening?" The words were on my face.

"What are you going to do?" she asked.

"Well, until I figure out what the heck is happening, I guess I'll stay up late and write some kind of sermon."

And so I did. I can't really remember what I said, and I'm sure it's been long since forgotten by those dear people who had to listen. A few weeks later some folks from the downtown church invited us over for dinner. After the meal, the man of the house looked over at me and said, "I will now tell you the truth of the matter. We did not understand who you would be and have never heard of the Duke Endowment so we figured you were some "hired gun" that our no-count preacher had hired. Our plan was to run you out of town, and then you walked in that first Sunday morning with that girl of yours (my wife), and I looked at Mildred and said, 'My God, he's just a boy.' So obviously we did not run you out of town."

Was he ever right? Not only was I "just a boy," I was an ignorant-of-how-to-do-the-job boy. That fact was confirmed the next Sunday when after preaching at the "city" church, I drove up to the new church that had been added to the charge. I could hear singing coming from inside, and standing outside was Tootsie Croone. He was smoking an unfiltered Lucky Strike.

When he saw me get out of the car, he dropped the smoking cigarette on the front brick step of the church and slowly put it out with his shoe. He looked and me and said, "You the new preacher?" Before I could offer some kind of answer he said, "Well, listen. We did not like those churches we were with last year. We do not like the churches we are with now. We have no use for the District Superintendent or the Methodist Church for that matter and really don't even need a preacher."

Before the smoke cleared from the smoldering cigarette, I put my hand out toward him to shake his and said, "Well then, I'm your man." He looked at me with a puzzled stare and told me to come in. So I preached my second sermon to those twenty-five people who gathered in the white-framed un-air-conditioned church sitting in between two cow pastures. The reason I remember the cow pasture scene is that often huge horseflies would swirl around my sweaty face as I preached. I mean, give me a break! I needed all the help I could get without swatting away these enemies from Satan or from wherever they came.

The next week I got a call from the local hospital informing me that it was my turn to be the volunteer chaplain for the hospital. I tried to tell the voice on the other end of the line that I was not the real preacher but she seemed not to care. It was "my turn."

So, I presented myself the next morning to the Ministerial Assistance Office and was given a stack or cards with names and room numbers on them. "These are people who listed no church affiliation. You are to visit them."

Needless to say, I was nervous and scared. I walked into my first room and there was a group of people huddled around a very old man who seemed to be shriveled up. His eyes were closed and he seemed to be breathing in a burdened manner. I did not know what to say. All I knew was that I needed to make a very quick exit.

With my mouth ahead of my confused mind, what I had meant to say was something like, "If you are in the same room tomorrow, I will come see you." What came out however, was, "If he is still here tomorrow, I will come see him." The family in unison turned in my direction with a look of great sadness. Of course, what they heard was, "If your loved one is still alive tomorrow, I will be back."

I turned and immediately retraced my steps to the Ministerial Assistance Office. I walked over to the desk where the woman who had given me my marching orders was still at her post. I tossed the stack of cards onto the surface of her desk. They scattered across the shiny clean space in front of her and I said, "Get someone who knows what they are doing. I am operating without a license."

I survived my ten weeks. The folks there either put up with me or kind of adopted "the boy," depending on how you want to interpret what happened. By the end of my term of "helping out" around the church I had discovered that I actually could write a sermon or at least I could put together some words and present them to those who showed up.

They weren't really sermons I suppose, but then neither was I a real preacher. Since this book revolves around the concept of covenant, it was obvious that the contract that the real preacher agreed to when he brought in the young hired gun was shady at best and an outright lie if looked at in the light of day.

I look back now and realize that my trial by fire and my learning-to-swim-by-being thrown-in-the-pool experience were the making of a really good story that you now know. If ignorance is bliss, I definitely had a blissful beginning.

God's Yes!

It was one of those years in which Christmas fell on a Sunday. For a local pastor, this is a bit of a dilemma: how to get people to come to church on Christmas morning? This particular congregation was even more problematic since so many of the members were young adults with children. What would it take to get the adults to get the children away from the Christmas morning "tree and present" ritual?

Not to be outdone, I tried every angle. I told my congregation first that it would be a come-as-you-are Sunday. Anything from pajamas to newly unwrapped sweatshirts would be allowed and welcomed. The next strategy was pragmatic, though a compromise. There would be no early service or Sunday School. We would have coffee for the adults and drinks for the kids, after which we would have one family worship service.

I had offered the easy path. I had appealed to their stomachs. There was only one base uncovered: guilt. So I told my folks, "Don't let Santa Claus cheat Jesus out of his birthday!" Now, every avenue had been pursued, and so I offered what I hoped would be the crowning argument. If they came, they would get to meet the Innkeeper and hear the Christmas story from his point of view. I had done monologue sermons before and this was my favorite one to do. The stage was set.

It was a joy to me to see so many families stream in on Christmas morning. For a pastor, this was the best present of all. With all due respect to ole St. Nick, it was good to see so many people who had remembered, for whatever reason, that it was the day of "the dear Savior's birth." We sang some carols. We gave each other a Christmas morning hug. We were together as the family of God. It was already a great day. But the best was yet to come.

I introduced everyone to the Innkeeper. Even though I was him and he was me, I liked this guy. I had put together a very human character who was frustrated with all the lies he had been listening to from people trying to get a room. Preachers know when their people are with them. You can tell by the expressions on people's faces. My folks were with me on this Christmas morning. They were with me in the greatest of all stories. They seemed to be listening as if for the first time. It was great. It was Christmas.

Then I got to the part where the Innkeeper heard a knock at the door. Here are the Innkeeper's thoughts that Sunday morning:

"Looking at all the people sleeping, even in the hall, I walked to the door to let the cool air in and my own hot air out. I was already angry before I got to the door. I had quit responding to knocks at the door long ago, but for some reason I went this time. I stepped over all those sleeping excuses and opened the door.

"There they were: A rather shabby looking couple. She was hunched over on a burro that looked like it was about to fall from its burden. Then I heard the most ridiculous story of the evening. This poor guy looked at me and said, 'Please sir, do you have a room? We have looked all over and my wife is about to have a baby.'

"I almost laughed in his face. I had heard it all now. Here in the middle of this enrollment did this guy really expect me to believe that he would have his pregnant wife out in the middle of this mess? Was I supposed to believe that his wife was about to have a baby?"

It was one of those moments, one of those moments when a preacher can hardly believe what is before him or her. There was a total, captivating silence. We were all in the Christmas story, and then it came. From the back of the Sanctuary came a shout . . . "Yes!"

The silence deepened. "Yes!" That simple word was held in the air for a cosmic moment. The Innkeeper sure stopped. At first, no one knew what to do. It was one of those quasi-uncomfortable church moments. Then, as if one by one people started realizing what had happened, the laughter began. "Yes!" The Innkeeper lost his character and everyone knew it. The pastor had forgotten an age-old secret: Do not ask a question in the sermon that can be answered easily by a child. They will answer.

Four-year-old Teddy Gellar had been listening more intensely than the others in the congregation. Christmas is after all a children's day. From his perch on the back of the pew, as soon as he heard the question, he simply had to exclaim the answer with much enthusiasm. Should we believe that into the midst of chaos and clutter, in the midst of lies and excuses, that a child was about to be born? "Yes!"

I turned behind me to a chuckling choir. I leaned against the altar table and said with a smile, "What am I supposed to do now?" As if I had said it to the whole congregation, the place erupted not with the gentle laughter of embarrassment but with the joyous laughter of childhood. It was a magical moment. The laughter lasted much longer than most sermon points are remembered. The laughter filled the room and the people. The laughter made people who needed to forget, forget. The laughter made people remember who needed to remember. It was a miracle.

The Bible says that "A little child shall lead them." On this Christmas morning, the prophecy was fulfilled, again. It took a child to answer the question. It took a child who did not know any better. It took a child to really listen as if for the first time. It took a child to want the baby to be born in spite of disbelief and uncertainty. It took a child to lead adults to God's answer for this world: "Yes!"

Thank you, Teddy. Thank you for showing even the Innkeeper what the answer to the question should be. Thank you for not holding back an answer that cannot really be held back. Thank you for showing the family, in such a real and vivid way, what Christmas is really about. It is God's Yes!

For those of you who might be wondering what happened to the Innkeeper who'd been lost for words, he did resume his story after a few precious moments of laughter. But he knew that the story had already been told in one word, "Yes!" A child had preached the sermon on Christmas day and I was glad simply to be there to hear it. "Yes!"

The Biggest Promise of All

ALL OF THE STORIES up till now have been about covenants made and broken. The covenants woven between these pages have been mostly implicit. There have been no contracts signed, no hands raised in solemn allegiance. The covenants in these stories have been the ground upon which the characters have walked. They are promises that are taken for granted, promises between relatives in a family, promises between husband and wife, promises between friends.

Most of the time, we do not need to write out our promises to each other. Covenants bind us that come with our birthright. We are intertwined by blood and by love. We are drawn together by something held in common. Even a house can be a sign of covenant as in "The Dwelling Place."

Covenants have to do with next-door neighbors, loving hands which shape us, relatives who either want to or have to take us in, and loving itself, which somehow encircles us in its arms. Covenant is what we all long for, and yet we run from these bindings when we think we need to be free. It is not human nature that takes us back in when we turn around and realize that we have run too far. Human nature would have us pay the price and go on. Covenant is there because we are individually too small to provide what it takes to love beyond the boundaries of our self.

I would like to share in this closing chapter some thoughts about the story that I believe shaped all of the characters in this book up till now. It is the story of a kind of love that could not rest until the lesson was learned. It is the story of the biggest promise of all.

Once upon a time, before there was time, God decided to make a world. This was not some idle endeavor; God had given it a lot of thought. God wanted someone to love back. There was just too much love to keep it all bottled up, so God created. And was it good!

There were gardens and animals and stars and marvelous bodies of water. One day God was looking into one of those very still bodies of water and saw himself/herself. Since God alone is allowed to be completely proud, God thought, "Gosh, I look good. I think I'll make some people in my image. Besides, I want someone around to enjoy all this I have created."

So, God grabbed some stuff laying close by and created a "he" and a "she." God realized from the very beginning that there needed to be both in the world, since the very nature of God includes both masculine and feminine.

God could not get over how fine the newly created two-legged creatures looked. They were, in fact, as naked as the day they were born, because they had just sort of been born and because their nakedness was lovely. This was before anyone decided that bodies were bad somehow.

God made it clear from the very beginning that these two people had an obligation to the earth. After all, God had used the earth to make them. They were literally "people of the earth." It was only later that God would have to remind people of that now famous phrase "from dust you came and dust you shall return," but I'm getting ahead in the story.

The covenant with Creation was made perfectly clear by the first object lesson. God knew that these two first people were a bit like children. Well, I mean they were, so to speak, children. Anyway, let's not ask too many questions of the story just now or we'll miss the point.

God took this first couple over to a tree and drew them a picture. Basically, there was a line drawn just in front of the tree. God said, "You see all of this garden? Well, it's all for your enjoyment. The only thing that you have to remember is to not take any fruit off this particular tree. Don't ask any questions. Remember, I'm God and you're not."

It was that simple. That should have been easy to understand. "Look; don't taste." God was saying that the tree was there to remind the people that they had in fact not made any of the garden and that this signpost was a graphic way to allow them to remember who it was that made the garden and them. God was saying, "Let Creation remind you of who you are and whose you are."

It did not take long for the two images to forget who they had been created in the image of. The tree looked so inviting, first of all. It did not help matters that one from the bad side had made a point of hanging out around the tree. This sly creature saw an opening one afternoon when the she was eyeing the tree: "Looks good, doesn't it? I'll guarantee you it tastes even better than it looks. I had one of them apples yesterday and look how shiny my skin is. This fruit is the finest of health foods. You won't believe what it will do for life expectancy."

The she was a sucker for such advertising. She put up some mild resistance that was no problem for this cunning creature. After a brief conversation about the benefits of an apple a day, the she sunk her teeth into the inviting fruit.

The first few bites were good. She took a few steps all the while chomping on the apple. Suddenly, she came upon one of the many streams that ran through the garden. She looked into the still waters, and what she saw made her drop the apple. For the first time she noticed that she was naked. She had never thought of this bare fact. She was instantly ashamed and did not know why. As she turned to run for cover, her stomach began to ache.

Later that afternoon, the he found the half-eaten apple and wondered why the she had left it laying on the ground. He guessed that it was the she that was guilty (which by the way was a new word on the scene) of littering when he found her hiding behind the fast-becoming-famous tree. "What the heck are you doing and why did you leave this half-eaten apple laying over near the stream?"

It was at this point that the expression "misery loves company" had its birth. The she quickly decided that whatever it was that was going on, she did not want to be alone with this feeling. "See if you think this apple is as good as I thought it was. I saved half for you."

Lies were becoming easy to tell all of a sudden. The he had never had any reason not to trust the she before. In fact, he had never really thought about the concept of trust. It seemed to come naturally. He took a bite.

In the background, there was applause. The sly creature who was hanging around the tree still had arms and legs so applause was called for. It was later that God grabbed the rascal up by those arms and legs and declared that from that point on, the creature could slither along on the ground rather than walk because of all the trouble this smiling low-life had caused.

The he soon developed the same stomachache and immediately thereafter ensued the first domestic argument. The he wanted to know why in the world she had done such a deceptive thing. The she said that he should have known better since he had always said that he knew more than she did anyway. The he did not remember ever saying such a thing but now that it had been stated, it sounded like truth to him. So let it be written, so let it be done. The he thought he knew more than the she. That part took a long time to see the light of day. Some folks still think it is true and forget to read the original story of how it came to be thought to be truth.

About this time, God decided to take a walk in the garden hoping to bump into the fine "images." Not finding them right away, which was most unusual, God attempted the first effort of a parent to call children home. Like many efforts since then, it did not work. God had to go looking for the pair.

Sure enough, they were hiding. Parents for generations have come to learn that when you say "what's the matter?" and the response is "nothing," another question must follow: "Come on, tell me. What's the matter?" This conversation will last exactly as long as the parent allows it to go on. Sooner or later there must be a bottom line.

The he fessed up first, hoping to get one up on the she by blaming her. This process became the very nature of things. The she did likewise. God whispered something like, "I should have known" and walked toward the couple with a not-so-happy expression. Before the day was over, the couple found themselves standing naked outside the garden. They quickly fabricated the first clothes since they no longer felt a part of the place and felt like someone was staring at them.

This was the first broken covenant. After this initial breach, the effort became second nature with the hes and shes who followed. The children of the first couple could not get along even though they were brothers. God had meant for there to be a natural bond between family members but these two proved that even God could not make everything run smoothly. One brother killed the other brother, mainly because of jealousy. This was the beginning of the first soap opera. After the murder, the one with blood on his hands found himself on camera with God, asking questions again. The script was clear. The brother asked that question which has been echoing down the years, "Am I my brother's keeper, or what?" To which God said, "What do you think?"

From this point on you could almost fast forward the tape because what follows is more of the same in about every variation possible. God first picked a certain tribe of people and said, "Look, I'm picking you not because you are so great but because I've got some special things for you to do to show the rest of the world what I am like. If you will listen to me, I'll promise you a bunch of stuff including some land, a code to live by, and most of all, my promise to be your one and only God. How's that?"

God kept his/her end of the bargain, but you guessed it, the hes and shes acted much like their original relatives and kept making bad choices. God sent some really special people to convey the seriousness of the big promise. Most of us have heard of these covenant conveyers. Their pictures have made their way into most Sunday School literature. Such folks as Moses, David, Miriam, Deborah, Isaac, Jacob, and many more have had their images attractively presented in all kind of Sunday morning fold-outs. After these initial famous people, God sent a series of reminder-type-folks called prophets as a kind of last-ditch effort to get the hes' and shes' attention. Most of these met limited success and some found out that working for God was the pits.

God's special tribe ended up in captivity at least twice in this history of broken covenants. Both times, even though God did not have to go after them, God did. God just could not let go of that original love that started the whole thing. The hes and shes seemed to be able to let go of it whenever it became convenient to do so.

Just about the time God figured that he/she had made a cosmic mistake by creating all this mess, God got a rather radical idea. How in the world could God finally convince all the hes and shes that this covenant stuff was at the very heart of the matter? One thing God had learned in all the experiments up to now was that the one covenant that seemed to matter most to the hes and shes was their bond with their children. Maybe, just maybe . . . naw . . . it was too extreme a measure.

After thinking over the alternatives, which included wiping things out in some fashion other than a flood (that had not worked before, and besides, a rainbow in the sky was God's way of promising not to do that again), God decided that the extreme was the only thing that would work.

God always liked surprises so when God did this final covenant-making there were a number of surprises in the script. First of all, this time there was no law book given nor demands made. This time the covenant came wrapped in swaddling clothes. God wrapped love in flesh. This conveyer of the covenant was not just a messenger about the covenant. This messenger was the message.

The phrase "only child" seemed to mean something to people. At first, they listened. God had learned a lesson from the past however, so God knew that things would probably not work out.

When the hes and shes killed this messenger, that was nothing new. That had happened before with other messengers whom God had sent, but this time the people did not realize that the message could not die. God simply raised the message and the messenger up from death. That got people's attention. Death was a pretty big matter with people since it seemed to happen to all of them, so when God announced that death was no longer a big problem, many people listened.

Jesus was the messenger and the message. He spoke about a new covenant. On the last night before he was done in, he had a meal with his special friends. When he poured out the last cup of wine, he told them it was a sign of the new covenant. He proved his point the next day when his blood was poured out at the bottom of a cross.

At the very instant when God's only child died, God stopped everything for an eternal moment. Some people standing close by thought it was an earthquake but what it really was was God's heart breaking. This message was at the very center of God's heart.

Some folks thought they heard thunder, but if they had listened closely, which hes and shes have trouble doing, they would have heard God say, "From this point on, I am making a new covenant with all people and this earth. I will not let my child's death be in vain. This is my blood which spills on this earth that I gave you. I promise that I will never leave any of my children who walk upon this blood-soaked earth. I also promise that since I have taken aloneness and pain and death into my very heart, I will redeem them."

All covenants now are incorporated under this special one that was made one Friday afternoon. If you look carefully you can see this covenant underneath all of our covenants. It is the biggest promise of all. It is the one that makes all the others matter.

Part Two

Poems about the Journey of Faith

I HAVE SHARED STORIES about covenants, which focus on promises kept and promises broken. Mark Nepo, a writer and poet, reflects on the spiritual journey that is the context for the need for covenants to be made.

In his book *The Book of Awakening: Having the Life You Want by Being Present in the Life You Have*, Nepo offers this reflection: "To journey without being changed is to be a nomad. To change without journeying is to be a chameleon. To journey and to be transformed by the journey is to be a pilgrim."

Many of his writings are poems. Poetry has been called "the language of the soul." What follows are poems I have written about the Christian journey. Many are based on Scripture and others are based on times that make up the Christian year or other events.

I offer these poems as reflections for the one who wishes not to be a nomad or a chameleon but who desires to be a spiritual pilgrim on the journey of faith.

Begin Again: Advent, the Dawning of the Christian Year

Not like the world
is this marking of time
For in our too many appointments
we find ourselves lost
in a desert of
dates and cluttered
calendars

We need another way to find
out when and where
we are
So, some long ago faith
ancestors created a
different way to tell time
a beginning before
the outside world's
beginning

This New Year greets us
from some wilderness
where a strange voice bids
us to prepare not
for confetti but for
repentance

"Begin again" is the invitation
from a calendar of faith
that asks us

to wait and wonder
rather than
rush toward a tomorrow
that is not yet

The time that lies ahead can
be but a marking of days
or
could it be a
journey of the soul
seeking a path
rather than a paved-over
toll road
whose price is
too high?

Advent's call is to again begin
with a keen awareness
that life is not marked by
numbers on a folded page
but is full of
days that are gifts
from the creator
of all time

Every Valley: A Poem for Advent

Based on John the Baptist's words in Luke 3:5.
Every valley shall be filled, and every mountain and hill shall be made low,
and the crooked shall be made straight, and the rough ways made smooth

Echoing against the walls of
the stale past
comes a voice shouting
the need for
something new

An old prophet needing
some resurrection in
our desert of constant
bad news carried
on air waves invisible
but so real

"There will come a child
to all of you who
feel so old because
of burdens that
seem never to be
lifted

Mountains of grief about
what could be
surrounded by valleys
of constant noes

But there is coming a
time when every
valley shall be
filled"

Prepare to welcome one
who longs to make
all things new
if we but surrender
our rigid pride
and constant need
for certainty

All children no matter
your age
listen now to a voice
crying in our wilderness

Every valley can
be filled
with a love
beyond this world

Advent means believing
what is unbelievable
Hearts can be softened
and old beliefs
given new breath

Every valley
yes, every valley
even yours
can be filled
O child of a soon to be
silent night
be born in us today

Why the Waiting? A Poem for Advent

Ask the caterpillar
as it spins
a place of waiting
as a forethought
of a coming birth

Why the waiting?

Prophets asked the same
of a God whose
time seemed too slow
for an impatient people
who felt forgotten

Why the waiting?

A frightened girl discovered
an answer
as mystical words
surrounded her in a
moment of surprise
She would hold
the waiting

Her journey would be
one of waiting
The announcement sudden
but not the birth

She would have to
ponder and wonder,
How could this be?

Now we must wait
and join her in
the pondering
The manger will be
empty without
our waiting
To rush such a journey
is to miss
the time to prepare

She would hear harsh words
that first long night.
"No room"
Let us not speak them
again into
her waiting

"Prepare him room"

No King but Me: The Thoughts of King Herod

Students of ancient texts
tell me of a
coming one

Dreams haunt me
for there is no room
for another "king"

My people's eyes are
full of empty hope
It must stay
that way

Rumors of some child
born under starlight
must cease

"King of the Jews" is
a solitary title
not to be
shared

His birth
I cannot stop
but
his life will
be short

There can be no
king but me
Still
why do my
dreams
bring fear?

Will They Listen to the Silence? A Christmas Poem

Forbidden fruit filled with
caution
in my
garden of plenty
but
they did not listen

Stone tablets imprinted with
laws of life
breaking
on my mountain
of fire
but
they did not listen

Shouts from prophets begging
even pleading
commanding
their attention
to be my people
but
they did not listen

So now I will speak my
Word
into a Silent Night
surprising
them with my

child
but
will they listen?

So many words have I
spoken
the loud desires
of my heart
So now
there will be
the soft cry
from a manger
and in the
silence
surely they will listen

Quiet the Storm: A Poem for Christmas

An explosion of light
ever so long ago
Creation's moment
as time began
amidst a storm
'Twas how it had to be
such power unleashed
as a garden grew
amidst the storm
and a voice offered
life that was death
Banished from a paradise
of wonder
we journeyed through
the storm longing
for a quiet that
would not be
Then came a mystical whisper
offered to a fear-filled
little girl
who in the midst of
the storm
spoke words of hope,
"Let it be"
A star cast light into
the midst of the storm
Voices of delight filled
a midnight clear

and our journey ended
next to a manger
Then God spoke as
the child slept,
"Quiet the storm"

'Twas the Night before Christmas: The Real Story

Here is something lighthearted I wrote years ago to read to children on Christmas Eve. It can be used in family times or in worship.

'Twas the night before Christmas
and all through the stable
not an animal was sleeping
None of them were able

Something special was ahead
all the animals knew
The cow couldn't speak
but she did say, "moo"

A star was shining
ever so bright
And the donkey was nervous
He was really uptight

The animals could sense it
but they really could not say
so they tried to keep warm
in the midst of the hay

If the sheep could have spoken
she would have shouted, "hoorah"
But in the excitement
it just came out, "bah"

Something was stirring
in the air that night
That special star was in the sky
shedding its light

Then out of the dark there appeared
such a clatter
The animals wondered
just what was the matter

The door slammed at the Inn
and the sign read "All Filled"
and the stirring of animals
was suddenly stilled

From out of the dark
came Joseph and Mary
It was time for a birth
and things were kind of scary

Some angels flew by
knowing the hour was near
and hurried off
to sings songs of great cheer

The first folks they found
were shepherds tending their sheep
but news like this
just was not going to keep

The angels broke into song
the sky filled with joy
and they told the shepherds
about the birth of a boy

"Hurry," they said
"and in a stable you'll see
the birth of your savior
It's the manger baby"

The shepherds had trouble
believing their eyes
It was angels they saw
so they all gave high fives

Meanwhile back at the stable
Baby Jesus did appear
way before the pawing
of tiny reindeer

Because it's Jesus
that gave Christmas its start
Before Santa and Rudolf
God gave us his heart

In a manger of hay
with animals for friends
Baby Jesus was born
That's the way Christmas really begins

The shepherds arrived
the wise men three
with presents at a stable
with no Christmas tree

So remember the night
animals wanted to speak
and come to the manger
for this child we must seek

Before mistletoe and Jingle Bells
before Grinches and shopping
came the meaning of Christmas
before we ever hung a stocking

So sing a song of good cheer
children in all times and all places
for little boy Jesus
came to put a smile on your faces

And as the curtain came down
the animals thought, "What a sight!"
and Mary and Joseph whispered,
"Merry Christmas to all
and to all a good night"

A Distant Knock: The Innkeeper's Story

Sleep was a friend that
night so full
Tired of disappointment
I no longer responded
to knocks
at my door

No fault of mine was
the forced assembly
My trade was to house
people not excuses
so my words
were clear,
"No room"

My retreat was the night
so in a dream I
heard a distant knock
Wanting not to awake
but I did
to find them

"with Child"
his words
waking my slumbering soul
What kind of man would
take this risky journey
into the unknown?

Wishing I had stayed dreaming
I led them to my stable
saying not what
was in my heart and mind
"What kind of world
must this be?"

Then in her pain she put
her hand upon my face
and whispered haunting words,
"Bless you dear one
You make space for
God's child
this night"

Her kindness contained no judgment
and her words wrapped
me like some blanket
Not ever have I felt
such an accepting
presence

I walked back to my
place of dreaming
wondering about that
distant knock
and what kind
of God
would do this

You Did Not Hear: Mary Holds Her Newborn

You did not hear
his cold words
"No room"
Sheltered you were
in the warmth
of my cradling love
Now I wrap you tightly
in bindings to
keep you from harm
but can I really
do so
O child from beyond?
What other rejecting words
will you hear?
Shepherds tell of
voices in the night
sending them to
kneel before you
Your eyes almost speak
that you hear
those same voices
a knowing gaze
that comes from
the one who sent you
to me
You will need to hear
those words of welcome
for I fear the
other voices
that will not understand

you and your ways
But for now, hear only
my soft song for you
"Sweet child of light
dream of love this night
For now you are only mine
In your eyes stars do shine
Share you I will one day
For now sleep quietly
in the hay"

Stars in His Eyes: A Shepherd Remembers

Another lonely night it was
tending a flock
unnoticed by a sleeping
village below
whose welcome we
were not provided

Outcast to them we were
thieves they thought
yet our wool gave
them warmth
for their cold
and aching bodies

Then the night exploded
with sounds from
stars that seemed to sing
inviting us to seek
one born in a stable
Why us?

So we went not knowing why
"To you this day is born
a savior"
Strange words for the lost
Were we to be found
by a seeking God
who forgets not
lonely shepherds?

Kneeling beside his manger
leaning toward his smile
I saw stars in his eyes
no reflection from above
but a shining from
within

The darkness, my darkness
would now have light
Could it be that the whole
world would know this?
Not just for me would
there be
stars in his eyes

Kneeling Not Where: A Poem for Epiphany

This poem is based on the visit of the wisemen to King Herod as they are on their way to see Jesus and their thoughts after arriving to greet the newborn King.

Bowing before a king who
knew not
not in some reverence but
with strange respect
Questioning were his words,
"Where is the new king
to be born?"
Motives of darkness
possessed he
Pleas to return with
new findings
hung heavy in the air
in our departing

Kneeling not where
we expected
Looking at his mother
looking at us
What kind of king is
this whose origin
is so lowly?
Still in our hearts we
felt deep truth
Gifts we bring

O Child of light
Somehow our darkness
diminishes beneath
the light of
your star

By the Lake: Jesus Calls His First Disciples . . . and Us

By the lake you called
Leaving nets
they dared follow
knowing not the path
and its narrow
way

You promised nothing
and everything
Emptiness would be first
to create space
for a risk that would
alter their lives
and ours

Now you come to our lakeshore
and offer us
your strange invitation,
"Follow me"
With empty nets we
wonder what help
we may be

In your eyes we see an answer,
"You are my hands
and feet"
But we are simply struggling

pilgrims looking for
a way
Yet you choose us and say,
"I am the way"

Follow Me: Jesus' Invitation

Your reaching hands offer
a daring invitation
"Follow me"
are words that hang
in the air
then grasp me like
some mystical rope
that pulls me
toward you

"Where will we go?"
I ask fearfully
But no answer comes
for part of the risk
is to simply follow
not knowing
except to take
the next steps
with you

"Everything will be changed
but mostly you"
are the unspoken words
heard only by
the ears of
my soul
"It is the journey that matters
not the destination"
words that shake the
fragile foundation
of my security

So I will follow for
those hands have
felt the piercing
of risking the unknown
and even death
was taken in by
your grasp
and defeated

On my own I feel
I would get lost
Your way is filled
with questions
but I will live with
the mystery
and trust that
in your hands
are the answers

A Pearl of Great Price: An Encounter with Jesus

An encounter with Jesus by a man who discovers a pearl of great price.
Based on Jesus' parable in Matthew 13:45–46.

All I had I gave
In looking for
the greatness of certainty
I found that
to discover truth
I had
to risk it all

Cedars of Lebanon
came to mind
but he pointed toward
a mustard tree
and smiled and
then spoke of small
being big

So in my search for true wealth
and many pearls
I found only one
but knew in my heart
it must be the only one
so I let go of it all
in order to
have everything

Then I held out my pearl
of great price
His hand cradled it
but for a moment
and then he returned it
to my waiting grasp

Then he spoke,
"Your little faith shall
now grow large
for my Kingdom's power
is in the hands
of those who will
glimpse the power
of small things
It is a pearl
of great price"

Thirsty: Jesus and the Woman at the Well

Thirst is deeper than our need for water. Spirits grow dry and weary when the deep needs of the soul are not met. Jesus encountered a thirsty woman one day at a well. She discovered, as we often do, that our thirst is for more than water. Based on John 4:5–30.

Dry and parched more
my soul than
my mouth
I wait for solitude
to come to the well
I need no more stares
from judging eyes

But even my thirst
to be alone
becomes dryer
by his presence
Can my loneliness not
be at least solitary?
This well is not deep enough
to draw water
for this
for me

I will acquire water for you
as I have offered
myself to other
thirsty men

leaving me empty
and dry
But you offer me water
not from
ancient cisterns
and you say it is
living water

And when I speak of ritual
to avoid your eyes
you look into my
empty soul
and I feel a cool
stream washing
away a dirty past

Who must you be
to offer such a gift?
Can you be the hope
we have forgotten
after long years
of waiting?

I cup my weary hands
and receive
your water
My thirst smiles
and suddenly
the noonday sun
seems not hot
but bright
in my darkness

I who offered water
for your thirst
am now filled
with something new

I will tell others
of this water
and of you
Many are they
who are thirsty

Words Too Much: Jesus' Beatitudes

Based on Luke 6:20–26.

Your words when spoken
were too much
or not enough
To be without and poor
feels to be un-blessed
yet you
offer blessing

Does my fullness keep away
your vulnerable love?
Those who have not
know their need
for what you
have

Hungry am I for a
food not present
and you offer manna
in my wilderness
"Bread of heaven feed me
till I want no more"

You say even my tears
are blessed
and noticed full well
by your father

counted as they fall
each a prelude
to a laughter
that awaits

Foolish says my world
are your strange words
too much and
not enough
too much for my
mind to believe
not enough for my
crying needs

And yet
you say if I but
risk to take
them in
I will be blessed

Your words too much
are the answer
to the world's riddle
And your strange wisdom
is the source
of a longing
never filled

You smile at my
struggle to understand
and as you turn
I hear you
whisper,
"Rejoice and be glad
yours is the
Kingdom of God"

Are You There? A Poem about Prayer

Have you ever wondered if God is listening when you pray? Jesus' story about the persistent man who knocks on his friend's door late at night in order to obtain bread for a visitor reveals the nature of prayer. The man knocking on the door learns that it is not so much what you get but who you get. Based on Luke 11:1–13.

I knock but
no answer comes
Are you there?
There is hunger to fill
with nowhere
to turn
It seems always late
especially when
I need you

I could turn away
from the closed door
but somewhere deep
inside my longing
there is the memory
of your smile
given to me in
a moment of
deep friendship

It is that memory that
keeps me by
the door
waiting

Just to know you
are there
is somehow enough
for now
bread or not
It is you I seek
and to know
you are there
and you care

Ah, a slight movement
of the door
and a shimmer of light
in the darkness
Whatever you give me
I will take
but the real gift
is
you

Stranger Love: Who Is My Neighbor?

Based on the story of The Good Samaritan told by Jesus in Luke 10:25–37.

Stranger love
says the story
No conditional
testing would do
Others passed by
protected by narrow windows
that kept them from
seeing the person
All they saw
was a label

Blinded by old expectations
they sought shelter
from the nearby pain
The space between
them and the
wounds of another
was more than
what was measured
by distance

They were apart due
to the safety of
hearts closed to
the reality of one who
would soon be called
neighbor

Stranger love saw only
the kinship that
was felt by compassion
The nameless victim was
after all
a stranger

So the one who told the
story in answer
to a question,
"Who is my neighbor?"
closed the distance
that separates our
tribal walls

Stranger love reveals that
the family of his father
is vast indeed
In some way we are
all strangers
walking a road
that might lead
to Jericho

Stranger love is what
is offered . . .
ours for the
taking

Angry Waves: Jesus Calms the Storm

"When the storms of life are raging, stand by me," goes the song. As we are sailing through stormy seas these days, I offer a poem about the thoughts of the disciples facing "angry waves." Based on Matthew 8:23–27.

Angry waves toss us
like leaves in
some storm
and
you sleep

So many unanswered questions
since that day
you bid us leave
our nets
and follow

Ravaged with uncertainties
is nothing new
for your words seem
strange even
to us

Storm clouds gathered
long before this day
as you spoke of turning cheeks
and loving enemies
and we sensed that
surely the rain
of doubt would come

You seem to care not
if we perish
either by angry waves
or floods of insecurities
about the future

And now you wake with
a look of disbelief
at our anemic faith
as if you did not
know well those
you chose

Looking past us or
perhaps through us
you gaze upon those
angry waves
and both within us
and around us
there is a sudden
calm

You turn and question
our too small faith
but if you want more
O Lord
it will have to
come from you

O master of angry waves
give us that
"more"
that we need
and we shall face
the upcoming storms
both within
and without

Why Weeds? The Parable of the Wheat and the Weeds

A poem asking why there is evil and suffering in the world. Based on Matthew 13:24–30.

Sunrise revealed their presence
uninvited intruders into
the beauty of my garden
"So from where did they come?"
I ask the Master
"Seems the *enemy* too
has a garden,"
as he turns away

"Then I will weed and destroy
the unwanted evil"
But he turns and says,
"No leave it for it
grows with the rest
and your skills
of sorting are poor"

Agreeing not I resist his
measured way
He notices,
"I am the one who will
harvest both
what you deem ugly
and beautiful
For now, know that the garden
is not yours
but mine

Living is done in
the midst of
the mystery of
the weeds
and those flowers
you long to gather

Only I decide
For now
garden as you can
not as you wish
All will be well
in the end
when I do the
final weeding"

On His Knees: Jesus Washes the Disciples' Feet

Thoughts of Simon Peter. Based on John 13.

We left nets hanging
and a father alone
Not for this did we
leave so much

On his knees he looks
up at me, those eyes
Not my feet, never
Rise up from such
a posture

We thought you a deliverer
not a slave to
wash dirt from feet

What kind of kingdom
is this where
towels are given
rather than chains
released?

I shall walk away from
such servitude
But your stare captures
me yet again
My words are dry in

my mouth as
as you say that
this is the way

What can change down there
on your knees?
Then you say that from there
you will be lifted up
But such lifting will
only bring you down

You hand me the wet towel
and bid me to kneel,
"As I do, do likewise"
and your soft smile
bathes my soiled
soul

So now, on my knees
I will again follow you
What kind of love
must this be?

Can This Save Us? A Poem for Palm Sunday

Thoughts of one in the crowd as Jesus enters Jerusalem
The word *Hosanna* means "Save us, now!"

"Hosanna" rings in the air
a large word for
such a small man
Sounding like some kind
of cheer
Does the crowd not
know its meaning?

Hosanna . . . "Save us now"
A plea from desperate
people tired of empty
promises not kept

But can this save us
arriving not on
some noble steed
but on a
tired donkey?

Some call him
"Son of David"
offering him a kingly status
but what kind
of rule does he bring?

Do we not need more?
What would God
be saying by
sending such a message?

Can this save us?

Crazy Religion: A Poem for Holy Week

Thoughts of Pontius Pilate. Based on Matthew 27.

Their crazy religion creates
empty Hosannas
that sound full
Promises for them have
been so broken
and their memories
long dead now
desire
resurrection

But there shall be no
new life in
their desert of hope
This surprising cactus
that appears to
bloom
will soon be
cut down

They think him some king
but he has no
kingdom, no rule
He forgets that he is
my subject always
his hands tied to
a reality he
cannot escape

Bring me water that I
may wash away
the residue of
their
crazy religion
I will once again kill
their longing
for a *more*
that
cannot be

It will be over soon
This premature sunrise
of dusty prophecies
The sun will set on
this crazy religion
And I can go home
and sleep
and forget

Bring me water . . .

Mining for Dust: A Poem for Ash Wednesday

We place a high value on gold but not on dust, which seems to get everywhere. But which does God value more? As we step into Lent with ashes placed on our foreheads, we hear the words "From dust you came and to dust you shall return . . . Repent and believe the good news."

Our hands reach toward
a shiny past hoping
to strike it rich
So we strain through the
dirt of our lives
to mine it for
a gold that
often eludes us

But the maker of it all
mines not for the
glitter of our world
Our God mines for dust
and through those
ancient hands there
is a sifting
for what is precious

As the earth makes gold
and we long for
its lofty worth
so the God who formed
the earth and its riches
cares not for the gold

but loves infinitely
the dust

The dust is God's gold
for into it the divine
breathed life's breath
And those old hands
shaped us into living beings
whose value is
much beyond
shimmering nuggets

And to sanctify it all
the old miner
of all Creation
sent the child of Bethlehem
to sift through
the rubble
and be dust
himself

Standing knee deep
in the running waters
of an ever-flowing stream
God Almighty reached
into the earth
and pulled from it
the dust
now gold

"From dust you came
and to dust
you shall return"
are the customary words
but when spoken by
God
they really say
"The dust is my gold"

God of Life and Death: Good Friday

We would love to skip Good Friday and rush to Easter, but we need at this time of waiting to know that you are the God of both life and death.

We need to know because
You are there when dreams die
You are there when jobs are lost
You are there when someone says, "I don't love you anymore"
You are there when our bodies won't keep up with our spirits
You are there when the prodigal child leaves home
You are there when the family pet
who understood us when no person seemed to
is buried in the backyard
You are there when we stand under the funeral tent
when we do not want to be there
You are there when we close our eyes each night
not really knowing if we will open them at dawn
And you will be there when we close our eyes
for the last time of seeing this world
so that when we open them in your new world of eternity
you can whisper to us, "I am the God of life and death"
We remember the time
your son was placed in that dark tomb
and we say thank you
Thank you
for you are God who takes in all of life
and even all of death
We await your resurrection promise
that overcomes all of our deaths.
Amen

Everything Waits: A Poem for Holy Saturday

Words still linger
in the early morning mist
"It is finished"
Those he called friends
are hidden away
and waiting
for they know
not what

A heavy stone covers
awaiting darkness
that now holds
one who claimed
to be the light

Tired guards wait for
morning light
so they may return
to yet another duty
to keep a rugged peace
that never seems
to happen

And the God he seems
to have lost
in the midst of
words of forsakenness
is waiting . . .
Waiting for what?

Everything waits this day
for tomorrow
all will be changed
The waiting will end
in a moment of
new beginnings

And the God who will be
found worth waiting for
will speak words to
the sunrise and say,
"The waiting is over—
arise my child"

How Can I Follow? A Poem for the Stations of the Cross

First Station: Jesus is condemned to die
Second Station: Jesus carries his cross
Third Station: Jesus falls the first time:
Fourth Station: Jesus meets his mother
Fifth Station: Simon helps Jesus carry his cross
Sixth Station: Veronica wipes the face of Jesus
Seventh Station: Jesus falls the second time
Eighth Station: Jesus speaks to the women of Jerusalem
Ninth Station: Jesus falls the third time
Tenth Station: Jesus is stripped of his garments
Eleventh Station: Jesus is nailed to the cross
Twelfth Station: Jesus dies upon his cross
Thirteenth Station: Jesus is taken down from the cross
Fourteenth Station: Jesus is laid in the tomb

How can I follow
your steps of death?
Your steep journey begins
with
"Behold the man"
and your fate is cast
with words of
condemnation

Waiting is your cross
lashed to your
already torn flesh
The weight of the world
placed upon
your bent shoulders

The seemingly weakened strength
of a father far removed
cannot keep you
from falling

You turn your thorny head
and bear witness
to the one who
carried you in
her now vacant womb
Her tears fall at
your soon to be
pierced feet

Stumbling next to you is
some stranger
who is forced to take up
your burden
You grant him a kind
glance for that is
all you have to give to
this cross bearer

Your muted rest is
not long
and a desperate woman
tries to wipe the blood
from your swollen face

She is brushed aside
like all the broken
dreams of the
chorus of women
who
can only weep and
offer sounds
of a grief that
is beyond words

How many times can
you fall while holding
all the darkness of time
on your weary shoulders?
Your lifelong
enemy laughs
for the angel of Hell
senses
a victory at last

Stripped of your few garments
and of the fleeting
words in that garden
when you pleaded to
be spared this
cup of poison
Naked now is your body
and even more
bare is your soul

The nails are not even
the worst of your pain
for the agony of watching
your Kingdom and its
subjects flee in
a darkness of
denial and betrayal
hurts you more
than the piercing
of flesh
The life in you drains
away and the
earth beneath shakes
in labor pains
not of giving life
but
of life being given

given for a world
that seems
not to care

You look up to a heaven
that seems quite empty
and your words of
forsakenness
are taken in by
storm clouds that have
robbed the sun
of its light

"It is finished"
is all you can manage
for suddenly
all of time ceases
and they take you down
and wrap you
in a cocoon of death
Finished indeed

One who at first doubted you
and who failed
to understand "new birth"
now gives up his own grave
so that at last
you may lay down
your dreams of
giving new life
to so many

So how can I follow?
But then I must
So I come to the
place of your slow
steps of death
It is the least I

can offer
To walk to your cross
with you
for me

Pieta: Mary Holding the Body of Jesus after the Crucifixion

This poem, a Good Friday meditation, was published in my book *Lost but Making Excellent Time: Transforming the Rat Race into a Pilgrimage.*

Playing as a child—that
day you fell against
the rocks on the
hillside of Nazareth
I held you as you wept
and watched the red
of life seep from
your wound

Now I hold you—fallen
again upon the rough
landscape of a world
not yet ready for you
O my son, how empty of life
you now are because
you were too full of
your father's love

Some angel's voice—now
so distant on this
tortured hill of death
told me of your coming
Pounding like nails in my
hearing is only your cry
of dying so alone
for heaven must be empty

Look what they have done—your
body so torn from the
hate you came to quiet
and now that quiets you
Some stranger offers you his
own tomb of death
for I have nothing to
give you but my tears

Death's Lament: An Easter Poem

So long have I kept watch
at a door
whose key
alone I possess

But now this upstart
divine avatar
dares rob me of
my prize

I watched as they stored
his broken body
in one of
my tombs
And once again
I slammed the door

And now
on this third day
a terrible sunrise
seems to burn away
my shadowy
power

O the sadness I feel
as he stands
there
in front of a
weeping woman
who sees him not

What shall I now do?
My hands empty
for I have laughed
so long
at their everlasting
defeat
all because of me

Now my lament is deep
for he is alive again
not so much for him
as for them

What is this haunting
word that
pierces my
heart
much as
his hands and feet
were marked?

Its sound frightens me
and now I sense
that
all will be
transformed

This word that changes
everything
that changes me
"Resurrection"

Dark for Three Days: A Poem for Easter

The light flickered for a
moment in time
only to be extinguished
with the words
"Why have you forsaken me?"

And then how dark it was
and a cave of death
sealed up the now
gone light
But the absent light
traveled far and deep
into the darkness
of a cavern
that would be Hell

For a time it seemed
the darkness claimed
victory
But this was no ordinary
light that lost
its radiance
This was the light that
caused suns to blaze
and gave stars their
reason to shine

And so on a day after
a tomorrow that some
thought would never be

the light overcame the darkness
and resurrection illuminated
the shadow of
death

O indeed it was dark for three days
but never again
will it be
The light of the world
took in the darkness
and sheer love
won

Easter was born in the
very womb of darkness
Still confused disciples
finally saw the
light for
who he was
It took three days
but now
forever has arrived

No Light in a Bottle: Lightning Bugs and Resurrection

Caught were they by
my childhood glee
The lightning bugs of
spring seemed mine
for the taking

One dark day long
ago another capture happened
Death bottled up the
light and sealed
the jar tight

Darkness held the light
and laughter prevailed
But the maker of
the light
would not have it so

For what was in the
jar was not
the tiny lights of
creation at play
in the evening

No, this was the lighting
of God's love
And there would be
no bottling up of
of this light

This would be no light
in a bottle
A clap of thunder
sounded and seals
were broken
and the light
of the world
was released

Resurrection is
loose

Running Toward Resurrection: A Poem for Easter

Thoughts of Peter and John as they run toward the empty tomb. Based on John 20.

I said I loved him, but then . . .
And it was I who said "never"
when the word
denial was uttered
Now we run toward a rumor
of what seems impossible

Empty was his burial
for we were
filled with fear
Some stranger's tomb
is his final home

Why do we run
when we should walk
slowly in our grief?

She said the stone
was rolled away
but that means little
for our faith too
has been removed

Ah, yes, it is empty . . .
So, they have taken him
away, again . . .

away from us
but then we deserve
such

Go back we must . . .
but could it be?
We ran toward resurrection
but we found nothing
But somehow perhaps
he will find us

Ah the nothing you found
dear disciples
means everything
for soon he will
find you
as today he finds us
It was and is
Easter
He is risen indeed!

Tired of Believing: The Road to Emmaus

The two disciples encounter the resurrected Christ. Based on Luke 24:13–35.

Tired of believing
we walked slowly
Heads and hearts weighed
down with grief
Longed for dreams
now dead
nailed to a post of hate

We wanted so much more
only to receive less
His words of hope silenced
by a tomb of death
And then rumors of
angel voices telling
of a sudden
emptiness

But we are tired of believing
so we seek rest away
from pain and doubt
You who ask questions
for which there are
no answers
Walk with us if
you wish
for we are lost
though we have a
destination

You offer words of promise
but we have forgotten
how to believe
Your words from a sacred past
have a strange
but familiar sound

Come in stranger and we shall
offer you the only
nourishment we have
for our souls are empty
Break the bread and offer
a blessing if you can
for we are not able
to bless anything

Your hands, they tell of
his story
Can it be that it
is you coming
to our tired
belief?

Do not leave
again
but then you must go
to find other
tired believers

Feeding Time: After the Resurrection

Thoughts of Simon Peter as Jesus prepares breakfast for him after the Resurrection. Based on John 21:9–19.

Haunting memories of the last
time he broke bread
Now those hands tear
another loaf
but it is my heart
that is broken

I deserve not this meal
nor did I deserve
the last one
It is not the bread
I remember tasting
but my stale words,
"I will never deny you"

My failure is as hot
as the coals
upon which you now
roast the fish
How can I eat that
which might fill
my stomach
but will never fill
my empty soul?

"Eat Simon, for you have work
to do,"
he whispers
But my appetite is gone
after those three
questions about
loving him

I am a crushed rock
that needs to sink
beneath the waves
So, I kneel before him
to beg pardon
But he offers not forgiveness
but a command,

"Now it is you who must
do the feeding
Peter
The past is done
I send you to a
future where
my sheep are hungry

Take this staff and
remember that
you too are a shepherd
Arise now
it is feeding time"

You Were but a Whisper: Mary's Thoughts after Jesus' Ascension

You were but a whisper
in the night
spoken into my fear
"It can't be"
were my words of
response to mystery

Moisture from my eyes
spoke louder than
my words,
"There is no father"
and then
the assurance
that you were
God's child

I held you first inside
before the harsh
refusal of "no room"
Soon I held you to
my breast
surrounded by
sleepy animals

I loved you as you grew
and longed to
keep you near
knowing that it

would not be
for you were never
really mine alone

Sharing you with your
Father and the world
was love's burden
and at times it was
as if the pain of my labor
revisited my memories
of you

You gave yourself away
on that God-forsaken
hill of hate
When they pierced you
I felt the pain
as I watched
the love bleed
from you

But you were not some
forgotten child
and the one who
first gave you
to me
raised you up
beyond even
death's expectation

Now those who loved you
not so well
tell of you becoming
part of a cloudy mist
as you
bid farewell

You will be remembered by
many and followed by

even more
But no memory will be
more precious
than mine
for I am and always will be
your mother

Needed Fire: A Poem for Pentecost

Based on Acts 2:1–17.

Sensing their anemic faith
he told them
to wait
"You will need fire
to warm the
cold of your past"

Returning to his father
he knew they would
be lost without him
so
he promised them
that a gift would
arrive to give
them needed power

They waited not knowing
in what form
the gift would come
And then came the wind
and the fire

None understood and strange
words came from
their still unbelieving
lips
Those who beheld it all

assumed too much
wine had been
spilled

And then came the calm
after the storm
Those who had failed
him so
rose to go forth
and alter the
world

The needed fire of Pentecost
burned away the fear
that they were
not the ones to
carry his cross to
a dying world

Needed fire for them
. . . and now
for us

Is That You? A Poem about Listening

Based on the Eli and Samuel story in I Samuel 3:1–11.

In the dark it came—
the word from an
old mentor
But his denial seemed
so sure

Returning to my darkness
I found it full
calling to me as if
my name was known
by a voice deep with
unknown meaning

Again, asking from where
the haunting words came
Now instructed to return
and offer a strange
but wise plea,
"Speak Lord, your servant
is listening"

Now in your own silence
it is time for
you to quiet the
stirring of your
too busy spirit
and wait . . .

Listen not just with
ears too full
Listen with a heart
longing for wisdom
After a pause so needed
you too can whisper,
"Speak Lord, your servant
is listening"

Never Alone: Who Will Separate Us from the Love of Christ?

Based on Romans 8:31–39.

The space between us
at times seems vast
But in some mysterious way
you are the space
Even my emptiness
is filled with
a quiet presence

When I feel alone
you know the solitary
place in my soul
for you created the
cave of my
unknowing before
I even knew

Perils around me speak
of your absence
"Never would you allow
such suffering
if you really cared"
comes the haunting whisper
in the darkness

Then your strong arms
hold me when
I fall

for only you know
the depth
of my longings

So when alone I am
never really alone
"Neither death not life, nor
height nor depth
nor anything in
all creation . . ."

So in the moments
of separation
there comes one whose
hands bear
the wounds of love
And with his stripes
we are healed

So when the waves of
vulnerability threaten
my drowning
your nail-scarred reach
pulls me from the depths

"Who will separate us
from the love
of Christ?"
Nothing in
all creation

When alone we are
never alone

To Have and to Hold: Wisdom from Above

What causes quarrels and conflicts? According to the book of James, it's those "constant cravings" within us. Here is a poem based on James 3:13—4:8. In these days of civil and political strife, we could use what James calls "wisdom from above."

"To have and to hold"
words uttered by innocents
in a moment of beginnings
But their meaning is
twisted as they
become a way to
possess life

Constant cravings capture
the light within
and all becomes holding
tight to feelings
and desires that lead
to always
wanting more

Seems it is the wisdom
of the world
though ancient words
tell of the foolishness
of it all
and of a fullness
that leaves us
empty

The Evil One smiles at
our "holding"
knowing that it distances
us from the One
who longs to free us
and grant us
true wisdom

"Draw near to God and God
will draw near to you"
Words that seem too simple
amidst the noise of
constant cravings
But in such nearness
is our freedom
And that subtle enemy
who longs to possess us
must flee
in the presence
of the ultimate
grasp of God
who whispers
to us,
"to have and to hold
from this day forward"

In the Light of Day: When Names Became Labels

Based on the story in Genesis 2:18—3:11.

In the light of day
faces reflect a
kind of brightness
that was meant
to be
in the beginning

But too soon shadows
appeared and darkness
revealed a creeping
sadness that
continues
even now

The Earth Being was
given the power
to name all
that was
but
names became labels

So now we reap the whirlwind
of our efforts to
control others by
putting them again
in the shadows
with our words

So east of Eden
having chosen
the lesser way
we continue our naming
Gay—Straight
Legal—Illegal
Black—White
Right—Wrong
Me—Other

Ah but in the light of day
we are none of
those labels
We are crafted dust
with a broken
memory

So again we need to
hear the call
coming in the
cool of the evening
"Why are you hiding?
Regain your nakedness
Be not ashamed
Cease the naming
You are simply
mine
in the light of day"

Go Where? The Faith of Abraham

This poem is based on Genesis 12:1, where God tells Abraham to leave everything and go to the land that God will show him.

Assurance is the warmth
of the evening fire
where stories are told
of a past
that is sure
Now you ask me to go
to the unknown
and I feel the cold
of uncertainty
with no map
You say I will be
like a father
granted a birth
and my Sarah
will bear labor pains
though impossible
But I am a stranger
to faith
knowing only what
is certain
and the comfort of
what is home
Your invitation echoes
with words that
proclaim that the new
can only be born
if I die to my

old ways
I will step toward
your dare
with the promise that
your steps are
ahead of mine
The word is new to me
"faith"
Where will its sound
take me?
The first step the hardest
for it is
away
I will go and perhaps
be the father
of something
greater than
me . . .

Naming Your Goliaths: Facing Fear

Based on the David and Goliath story in I Samuel 17:32–50.

Too young, too small, too foolish
All around voices
saying, "It cannot be"
But with a sling of faith
the too small boy
stepped into the
valley of doubt

Other armor did not fit
for worldly protection
was not the need
Courage grown while
guarding sheep
would be his armor
and faith

Smooth stones of risk
would be enough
eliciting laughter
from the
giant of disbelief
Against all odds
the enemy, fear
fell at his feet

So now we face our Goliath
Again, the peril of defeat

stands over us
casting a giant shadow

Pebbles of faith
seem of little use
but pick them up
and remember
God can use
what often seems
too small
to accomplish
great things

Step toward the fear
Name your Goliaths
What seems too large
can be faced
with what some say
is too small
And the God of David
will whisper,
"It will be enough"

The Shaping: Those Whose Hands Shaped Us

Family legend has it that my Aunt Hattie literally shaped me. It seems I was born with a huge knot on the top of my head causing my father to say the first time he saw me, "What's the matter with the boy's head?"

So, on hot summer evenings in delta Mississippi, my Aunt Hattie would whisk me away alone to my grandmother's screened-in front porch. She would rock me while pressing a warm cloth to the crown of my head. While she rocked and pressed, she would sing songs of her past to me.

My head and my life are now different due to the warm touch of love. Oh, I still can feel a small knot if I rub my hand over my now bald head, but still, it would have been more prominent if not for the one who took the time to shape me. Who helped shape you?

Looks of surprise were
present as viewers
witnessed the knot
on my head at birth
The result of a long labor
by the one
who gave me life
Noticing with love
the outgrowth of birth
My Aunt Hattie
took it into her hands
to shape my future
Knowing that heavenly hands
had sent me her way
she knew that it was hers
to do some altering
to aid the Divine
a sort of finishing

On sultry summer evenings
she alone cupped
my tender head
with hands and love
shaping me as she
sang lullabies whose
tunes were part
of her own shaping
Now I am who I am
due to the touch
of one who cared so
Her smile now faded
is seen and felt
in the portal
of my soul
And now while alone
I sometimes rest my hand
on the slight rise
on my head
and know that I
have been shaped
by those who loved
me when I
knew it not
Whose hands shaped you?
Close your eyes
and remember
Even if you do not
it will come
in the silence
for hands of the past
are always there

God's Parenting: Hosea 11

This poem reflects what I imagine are God's thoughts as a parent.

I see you are afraid
again
So many times
when all is going well
you forget
It saddens me when you do
I do not like being taken for granted
Parents have feelings too, you know
Sometimes I feel like locking you
in your room
and throwing away
the key

Then I remember
what you do not
I recall the days I held you
when you took those first breaths
I remember how I looked
into those tender eyes
and I knew I brought you forth
and as you grew
there were
those times you wanted to
go your own way
You acted like you no longer
needed me

But I will not give you up
even in those moments
when you seem to give up on me
No, I am God and not you
You will always be my children
and yes, I know
you are afraid just now
I feel your helplessness
as you face this strange darkness.
No matter how old you think
you have grown you are
and always will be my children.

I know the valley of shadows
and I will hold your hand
as you travel its ways
And when I hold your hand
I will remember it was I who
first taught you to walk
I will hold you
and your fear
and I will remember
how I held you
in those first days . . .
and I will smile

Dry Bones: A Poem for All that Divides Us

A poem based on Ezekiel's vision in Ezekiel 37:1–14.

Again, the valley waits
before us
Parched, dried up hopes
Dreams stripped
of life

Words no longer speak
For the arid wind
of anger and mistrust
fills the crevices
between us

Dry bones lay still
black/white
gay/straight
us/them
right/wrong
"Can these bones live again?"

Then a whisper is heard
somewhere between
our breath and the
one who breathed
it into us

"Prophesy to the breath"
A strange request
but not to do so

leaves the valley
stale with death

As long as our vision is
captured by dry bones
there will not be new
life and our valleys
will be ruts
that become graves

But the life-giving breath
of the Lord
can make dry bones
live again
and people will no
longer be the
skeletons of
our labels

"Put flesh upon the bones"
says the wind
and your dried-up
words
can breathe again and
you may walk
together in a valley
of life
not death

Stillness Afar: Psalm 46

From long past words echo
in a valley of questions
an ancient whisper
from one who knows
all,
"Be still and know . . ."

But my longing is too full
and the quiet you offer
seems beyond my
striving to always
be someplace else

"Be still and know that
I am . . ."
My restless soul wants
to listen but my doing
outpaces my being
too tired to
even try

But you do not cease your plea
as if you know the
emptiness of my wearying
ways to arrive
and finish what will
never be complete

"Be still and know that
I am
God"

You announce the "why" of it all
To be still is not just for me
but for you
To listen to the stillness
is to know
you

"Be still and know . . ."

Tender Love: Mother's Day

In memory of my mother and in honor of all mothers.

That day you held me
wet with my tears
I begged you to not take
me to some stranger
So with needle and thread
you stitched my
bleeding knee

Now the scar so beautiful
and old reminds me
of tender love
so often given

You sang of bluebirds
flying through gardens
And tiny spiders that
climbed spouts
only to be washed away
by words and rain

You struggled with a body
that would not aid
your spirit that longed
to love and give
But the limitations of flesh
could not hold back
that tender love

One evening after yet another
feast from your table
you sat in that chair where
so many songs were sung
And while reading some book
that would never
be finished
you slipped away to another world
where bluebirds and spiders
play forever

You are missed dear mother
But, oh you are not
forgotten
For your tender love
resides in me
and those
I love

He Called Him Father: Father's Day

Remembering that Jesus called God "Abba."

Mary's words seemed strange
as her son wondered
about the word
"father"

"He is but he is not,"
she whispered
"It matters not for now,"
was her consolation

As he grew in stature
and in wisdom
he leaned upon Joseph's
tired shoulders
and they both smiled

Soon he would discover
his other father
He told his followers
that like children
they should pray,
"Our father . . ."

But in a lonely garden
one dark night
on his knees like
a sad child
he spoke tender words,

"Abba, can this
cup pass from
your child?"

Hearing no answer
he simply bowed
and said,
"It is done, my father
Now all will be
your children
as I am"

So on this "Father's Day"
I who am a father
pause and ponder
that the God of
the cosmos
is one we call
"Abba"
because of a
very special
child

A Birthday Poem

I wrote this poem to celebrate my 72nd birthday on June 3, 2019. As you read it remember that you too have a birthday. It is based on Psalm 139:15–16.

O Lord, my frame was not hidden from you
when I was being made in secret,
intricately woven in the depths of the earth.
Your eyes beheld my unformed substance . . .

Waiting was I but knowing not
what would be
In that cosmic pause
you but took a breath
and
shared it with
me

Now filled with life my
eyes beheld new light
Months of sheltering darkness
now a memory
not to
be
remembered

In time before time you
were there
while I was
being made in secret
a weaving of your
own pattern

On this day of birthing
remembered
I whisper with that
breath you gave me
a small word
with deep meaning,
"Thank you"

For I know that when
that breath
leaves me
you again will be there
weaving something
new
A wonderful kind of
birth beyond
life

Ah Freedom: A Prayer for Independence Day

The land of the free
words from a song
and even as they echo
in the air
one wonders who is
free

Blood-stained beaches
are haunting reminders
that freedom is more than
words in creeds
or mottoes on
walls

Our land of the free has
a complex past
still sometimes chained
to a dark memory
where slaves sang
sad songs

But every family has to
learn from its past
O God of all, help us
turn toward the
light that you love
to offer

Ah freedom
It should be

for all who breathe
'Tis a gift not to be
of slight but cherished
and held
with reverence

My freedom is linked to
yours indeed
for above our waving flag
there waits a Creator
who longs for all
to be able to whisper,
"Ah, freedom . . ."

Patience: The Thoughts of a Caterpillar

In light of the need to practice patience in our fast-paced culture.

Wanting so to go forward
yet the stillness
pulls me to stay
Waiting seems unnatural
yet natural
The next place beckons me
but to rest in
some spinning present
betrays a speed
that would be my end
not a beginning

What is this quiet voice
within my colorful self?
It speaks to an outside
world of a need
to not hurry so . . .
Creatures of a larger place
going so fast
walk by
not noticing
a pattern of wisdom

So I shall wait upon
a longing not understood
but true
The wind upon the leaves

speaks of another
world that waits
upon my waiting
I shall dream of it
and wish some day
to fly

Into the Space: For Those Who Grieve

Into the space where
love dwells
there comes a robber
who dares to
steal life
He smiles as he leaves
us in the wake
of a tide that
seems so
final

But there is one who
has traveled the
valley of grief
and loss
He too smiles for he
faced the robber
one dark Friday
and
but a few days later
he took back what
had been
stolen

Death held tight to what
the prize might be
but the Lord of life
cheated him
of
his victory

So now for all of you
who grieve
the loss of love
Reach out to a hand
that reaches
to you

It is the wounded hand
of the one
who faced the darkness
and who now
offers you the light
that cannot be
vanquished

The one you lost is
not lost to
him
His never-ending love found
the one you loved
And into that
Space of what seems empty
Resurrection fills
it all

The Horizon: For Troubled Times

Above
the darkness
of present reality
covers me like
a cold blanket
My steps are slow
and sad

But as I look toward
an edge of light
there comes a kind of
invitation
"Walk on, O child
of the earth"

So I step gently
in the direction
of the welcoming
"There is always light
in the darkness,"
the wind whispers

"Look not just to
dark clouds above
The horizon is your
destination
not today's
sorrows"

So with that same wind
of hope
at my back
I walk toward
the light

"Is the light setting
or rising?"
I ask
"It matters not,"
the breath of life
tells me
"The light of the
horizon
is for your
beginnings and endings

Take heart and remember
ancient words . . .
The light shines in
the darkness
and the darkness
will never
overcome it

Walk toward the horizon"

A Great Cloud of Witnesses: Those Who Helped Form Us

A poem based on Hebrews 12:2, acknowledging that our faith
was formed by those who came before us.

At times my faith holds me
when the ground that
should be firm
seems to quiver
But all is because others
first held
that faith

I am the birthing of a
labor of testing
by those who first faced
trials long past
They endured and
in so doing
left a legacy
which now surrounds
me

"A great cloud of witnesses"
I can almost breathe in
their prayers
Some were not for me
but lingered
awaiting my need

My journey began with them
and when the noticing came

they looked my way
and bathed me
with their past
and their faith

When my spirit's vision dims
there seems a light
shines in the darkness
of my fear
It is some deep assurance
that holds me
from beyond

Ah, a great cloud of witnesses
May I become
part of it
someday

Saints Everywhere: All Saints' Day

Colorful windows capture
their past
Frozen in time they look
down at us
our gaze transfixed
on their mighty
acts
And so the distance grows
between what they did
and who we are
Our limits are vast
and our humanity
a barrier to
the path they
took
Ah but such thoughts
are mere excuses
since the God who made
them to do great
things
made us too
and from heaven's
distant shore comes
a plea
"Serve me with all your heart
and you shall be
in the window of my
love for you
Greatness starts small
with acts of kindness

that are often not noticed
except by
me
Those you love
who seem lost to you
are found in me
for they passed through
the valley of shadows
their faces now
full of light
They too thought themselves
not to be saints
but their lives were mine
in their birth
so their death
was but a new
beginning"
So gaze upon colorful windows
but remember
the seeds of sainthood
are scattered by those
who choose the higher
way of servanthood
And when you do
from beyond those windows
their God and yours
will whisper
"You too can be a saint"

The Rest Is Light: All Saints' Day

This is a poem I wrote for All Saints' Day. I was inspired by the recent discovery of a gamma-ray burst from a star that exploded more than 13 billion years ago. The light from that explosion, traveling at the speed of light, arrived on the scene in 2009. I thought of this in the context of the phrase that comes from the Commendation that I use at the end of a Memorial service. I offer these words as I commend a person's soul to God: "Let perpetual light shine upon them . . . and may they be granted everlasting rest."

Some distant star
its source so
far removed
Yet it is here
now present in
our dark sky
Its radiance created
in the womb of
a distant birthing
But its light is in
the eyes of
our beholding
this moment

For the One who knows
the light also
holds the darkness
Our need is deep for
the shining hope
that in the dark
there is presence

And so when we let go
of our breath
that is life
we are promised rest
that is deeper
than the darkest
night sky

"Let perpetual light
shine upon them"
echoes in the dark
And the wound-born
words from the
tomb now empty
says
the rest is light

The Mountain Climbers: For all the Saints

I had been asked to do a memorial service at my 45th High School re-union for those in our class who are no longer with us, those who had "climbed their last mountains." It was an interesting evening. Wow, those people got old somehow.

We looked at a power-point show of "the Ghosts of High School Past" as we ate our food and chewed on memories. My old girlfriend was there and I spoke briefly with her despite my dear wife's accusation that I had flirted with her at our last reunion. I figure we are owed a few reflections from the past. After all she was the first to break my heart. Yes, she fell for an older guy while on a beach trip. She ended up marrying the guy, but all I remember is the deep ache that was new to me at the time.

The ache started somewhere below my stomach and came up around my windpipe, then seeped into my chest. It was a strange feeling. I did not know someone could do that to someone else. I had only played with feelings until that point. What was this sensation that felt like a roller coaster going down and not coming up?

So how do you describe a broken heart? Anyway, I lived, even though I thought for a while I would not. Sure, we all can laugh now about those first love downdrafts but it sure was not funny then. So, all that rushed by as I listened to her tell stories of her grandchildren.

But, back to the "saints." I conducted a brief memorial time for those names that were below the pictures that were mounted on a board in front of us. The pictures were from the High School Annual. They all looked so young and so hopeful and now they were memories. They were gone from our midst. It was a somber moment in the swirl of laughter and surprise at how we have changed.

This is the poem I wrote to read to my classmates that day. It is based on the song that many of us had sung just before graduation, a song of both hope and desire: "Climb Every Mountain." I share it with you for those of you who read these words and have climbed your mountains and discovered your valleys.

We sang of mountains
that could be conquered
With our knapsacks full of
hope we set out
Maps and charts were not needed
for at first we were
full of hope
that needed only time

But soon we found that mountains
have valleys between
their rugged peaks
so we stopped our separate
marches and joined
hands with another or many
For in our days
of youth we dared
not ask about
the fear of mountain climbing

So today we gather to smile
even about the tears
For remembrance is our tool
that we strike into the side
of this yet another peak
that we call "reunion"

And as we stand beside this
slope of a past whose
story is much bigger than
the simple song we sang
we step into a sacred silence
as we hold in our hearts
the names of those climbers
who are beyond the
range of our gathering
but

who are not lost to the
One who made all mountains
and who transverses all valleys

Hold on to them
O God who listens so well
to songs of youth
but who knows how quickly
hope can be swallowed up
as pilgrims on the way
discover their need
for ropes and charts and
you

So we hear their names and
speak them tenderly
from yet another mountain
that we climb this day
Hear them O God of all knowing
and complete
their lives that are
so sacred to you

Woven in the Depths: A Poem for Thanksgiving

Based on Psalm 139.

You did not appear on
some doorstep
ordered via
Amazon Prime

No commodity are you
for you were first
dreamed of
and formed
by hands unseen

Ancient words tell of
you being crafted
and woven in
the depths of the earth

And all those who breathe
in this mystery
who surround you
this day are living gifts

So at this time of pause
give thanks and
close your eyes
to remember who you are

You are "fearfully and
wonderfully made"

not shipped
but woven
not ordered but
crafted

O yes, give thanks

Falling Leaves: A Poem for Thanksgiving

So colors fall to the ground
releasing spring's hope
in a kind of death
spiral, but in the
breeze that
cradles them
comes a
leaf's whisper:

"Thank you for life—that
gift you offered me
to shine for a time
and twist in
the wind of
your breath that
first gave me
life"

So, in this season of color and endings
stand below one of
Creation's leafy canvases
and allow falling
life to surround
you for a moment
and then say,
"Thank you"

For we too are full of color
and life but
so often forget from

where we came
thinking we are
just here
in some
space

So, it is a time of falling
leaves that calls to us
a reminder that
we too are full of
a gift that
comes from the breeze
Hold a fallen leaf
in your hand and
give thanks

I Dreamed You Up: A Poem for Thanksgiving

I dreamed you up
Before you had thoughts
I thought of you
Your design came on the wind
a pattern of my making

The breath you first took
came when I whispered
your name before
it was given by
others

Your purpose in being
is to reflect me
You are not a product from
one of your stores
You are mine
and always
have been

So in this moment of pause
close your eyes
and ponder the why
of your life
You did not just happen
You are part of
my yearning
to give

Some try to name me
but I am beyond
your words or pictures
I am all that is and
all that
will be

Know this—you are loved
so yes, I will
accept your gratitude
It makes me smile to
know you remember
that
I dreamed you up

With this Breath: A Poem for Thanksgiving

With this breath I whisper
words of my forgetting
For memory fails me when
I reach back
to my beginning

You were there in that
moment of mystery
when life filled my frame
and Spirit poured
into my being

So many breaths I have
taken without notice
But now I pause to
remember from where
life came

You must smile at our time
of "Thanksgiving"
for you remember what
we so often
seem to forget

We are an extension of
your love for us
Our breath is from you
and our life
is pure gift

O God of all Creation
with this breath
we say,
"Thank you"

The Strangest of Kingdoms: A Poem
for Christ the King Sunday

Traditionally, Christ the King Sunday is the final Sunday of the Christian Calendar; it is the Sunday before Advent begins. It reminds us of God's reign over all things, despite the apparent chaos of this world, and challenges us to risk joining in with God to help bring about God's Kingdom on earth.

Whispered from the lips
of a lost soul
one final plea,
"Remember me when you
enter your kingdom"

And from below your
crown of thorns
your words bestow a
parting gift
to a dying thief,
"Today you will be
with me
in paradise"

At your feet your mother
remembers your beginning
one not fit for a king
with animals as
your only subjects

While a world slept
your strange kingdom
was herald by
mystified shepherds
who knelt before you
having heard voices
from the stars

What kind of kingdom will
remain as you die
forsaken by
the one you came
to honor and serve?

Will your rule die
with you
as you utter words
of forgiveness
into the faces of
those who placed
the crown of pain
on your head?

A strange kingdom indeed
Who will dare risk
joining its ranks
after your breath
leaves you
and will you even be
remembered as
a king?

Time to Sleep: Winter

Winter is not my favorite time of year, but the thought came to me that we need all the seasons of the year.

Blooms of spring now
hide from view
Muted shades of winter
will rule
Frigid winds sing a
song of sleep
It is resting time
for all Creation

A sacred text proclaims,
"For everything
there is a season . . .
A time to be born
and a time
to die"

So is this the season
of dying?
Nature seems drained
of its color
Life appears to seek
a time of withdrawal
Some kind of dark
ending . . .
and yet

Faith whispers,
"Be patient
As a divine cocoon
spins a necessary
blanket
even Creation needs
a time to sleep
Wait for the
season of awakening
A rainbow of colors
will soon appear

For now, breathe deep
the cold air of winter
Resurrection is not
just for spiritual pilgrims
it is planted in
all Creation"

You Wait: A Poem for the New Year

Like hands bidding me
to come and see
you offer me again—
time

What shall be
even you do not know
So like some child
you say,
"Come play"

This life is not some
commodity ordered
from a warehouse
far away

And yet it is a gift
not arranged by
my hand but
crafted by
another

So, I step gently
your way
not knowing but
believing
And I hear you whisper,
"To live is grace"

Step Forward . . . Slowly: A Poem for the New Year

Ah, there you are with your
arms wide open
You bid me to step forward
slowly
Your hand raised as a caution
to guide me
for you know
my desire to run

You know me because your
memory has witnessed my haste
times I should have walked
open eyed
Instead, I have hurried to
arrive only to
find myself
weary from the journey

So, you are new, again
and you offer fresh hope
if I see instead of
just looking
How much did I miss
in your past offerings
because of my
haste?

You want me to make it
better for all
not just for me and mine

You wait
as I must before I start to
run . . . again

And what is this you whisper
to me in my waiting?
"Make it truly
the gift of a new year
. . . this time"

Shall We Take the Darkness In? Boston 2013

This poem is a response to the bombing that occurred at the Boston Marathon on April 15, 2013, when three spectators were killed and more than 260 people were wounded.

The darkness cuts into
our souls
like some switchblade
stuck into our gut
in the back alley
of doubt

Its hiddenness covers us
like a moldy blanket
cast over our heads
The smell of it is
rank with crowded
grief and hate

We bleed and we gasp
for again
the darkness seems so
vast and deep and
we remember not
the light

And that is the victory
that must not be
For light and life
are above and below
the lie that
is the darkness

We must tie off the wound
with torn rags
of love and compassion
and cast flowers over
the decay of the
wrong that wants to win

The darkness only wins if
we take it in
Its desire is to have
our souls, but our
souls belong
to the light

The darkness cannot stand
the flowers
that grow in the
ruin that becomes
the soil of new beginnings
and
it cannot believe that
our scars are the
signs of our healing

The darkness cannot win
unless we take it in

Goodness is stronger
than evil

Bear Arms or Bare Arms: Parkland 2018

I wrote this in response to the one-year anniversary of the Parkland shoot-ing. On February 14, 2018, a gunman opened fire at a high school in Park-land, Florida, killing 17 people and injuring 17 others.

Harsh voices will again shout
across aisles of divide
Tears on one side
and a call for
"the right to bear arms"
on the other

But then there will be empty
bare arms yet again
of weeping parents
and the young who witnessed
yet another
slaughter
of the innocents

"It will not make a difference,"
say those who hold
to that
ancient "amendment"
But those who now have
empty bare arms
that can no longer
hold
lost children
say through their tears

and grief,
"But can we at least
make a statement?"

It seems our "rights" have
over-reached
our vision to
give up something
so that
we may again gain
some sense
and a heart that can be
broken
rather than a
mind that
can't be challenged

Bear arms
and bare arms
and voices not
heard

So Why Am I Crying? John McCain's Memorial Service

While watching John McCain's Memorial Service in DC on September 1, 2018, I found myself full of tears wishing that our divided country could find some of the spirit that was in the Washington National Cathedral that day.

So divided we are
and yet
there they were
all lined up
next to each other
like maybe
it is supposed to
be that way

Presidents all, of
different colors
and stripes
competitors for
a season
but now
united in grief
and honor

What have we become
all hiding in
our prideful tribes
afraid that
someone or anyone
might "tread on me"
or get
something undeserved?

Can we find the good
that rests beneath
the need to win
and gain notice
so that we
will be
right while
others are wrong?

God, you were there in that
room listening
to all those noble words
about a man who wanted
more for our nation
not less
Please whisper into
the stopped-up ears of our leaders
to clear away the
clutter of "me and mine"
and find a
new way to
"ours"

Rest in peace, John
but haunt us
with your restless presence
that stirred within your
wounded chest
You and the God whose
face you now see please
come visit us
with a new vision
that allows us to
again see
what true
greatness is . . .

Shelter in Place: O God, Our Help in Ages Past

Shelter in place, they say
New words for
all too busy people
But there are other words
not new but old
that tell of
another place

Those words proclaim a God
of ages past
who offers hope for
years to come
Old words that
offer another kind
of shelter

Time goes so slow as
we wait and hide
from an unseen enemy
whose reach seems
all too far

But time is not measured
in minutes or hours
by this "ancient" God
for
"a thousand ages in
thy sight
are like an evening gone"

So, we who seek to
abide in the shadow
of your wings
shall seek that other
shelter
and this time when we
utter the words
they will not
just be words
but a prayer . . .

"O God, our help in ages past
our hope for years to come
Our shelter from the
stormy blast
and our eternal home"

A Strange Exile: In Response to Social Distancing during Coronavirus

A poem based upon Psalm 137:1–6, which refers to the time when God's people found themselves in exile in Babylon. They asked, "How can we sing the Lord's song in this strange land?" Since we often find ourselves in our own strange land, I share these words with you.

Long ago your people wept
by strange waters
They hung up their instruments
of music and praise
Tears were their bread as
they ate a meal of
fear and grief

Their voice seemed lost as
they lamented,
"How shall we sing
the Lord's song
in a strange land?"
Yet they answered their own question,
"Our tongues shall
sing anyway
for we must"

Now we are again beside
strange waters that
threaten to offer poison
Ours is an exile caused by
an unseen enemy

Again, we ask
"How can we sing
when our voice has left us?"

But if we listen
it is you who whispers,
"Yours will not be the
first song sung
into the darkness
Listen again to my song
offered to those
who felt lost,
'Fear not for I bring
you good news of great joy
for all people
There is now a savior'

He was born into the darkness
and he is born
today into your darkness
So sing because of . . .
Sing in spite of . . .
As he left he said to
those who needed him most,
'I will be with you
till the end . . .
I promise . . .
Do not be so afraid
Sing into the darkness
Sing the Lord's song'

I will listen for your song
as I listened long ago . . .
Sing"

The Story of Your Life: An Epilogue

Its beginning was before you
words of hope spoken
beyond your hearing
while you waited
in a womb of love
You are not here by accident
You are the answer
to God's longing
for stories to be told
so your living is all
a narrative of
light and dark
Listen well to other's stories
The noise is great
and easily lost is
the meaning in
poetry and prose
but it is there
if attention is paid
One day the last line
will be penned
and when breath
is gone
you will look back over
the chapters
and know that
we are all
living stories